Piece *of* Mine

Piece *of* Mine

PHYL ANDERSON

iUniverse, Inc.
Bloomington

Piece of Mine

iUniverse books may be ordered through booksellers or by contacting:

iUniverse
1663 Liberty Drive
Bloomington, IN 47403
www.iuniverse.com
1-800-Authors (1-800-288-4677)

ISBN: 978-1-4759-5188-2 (sc)
ISBN: 978-1-4759-5189-9 (ebk)

Printed in the United States of America

iUniverse rev. date: 11/15/2012

Introduction

E veryone has a story to tell. Some people feel their stories are great enough to write them on paper to share, while others keep those stories all for themselves. I believe every story should be told and shared. If anyone has ever lived, they have a story they should tell. Every story should be read by someone, not to imply that someone should read every story.

My mother used to have a saying in an effort to correct some of my "nasty attitude and funky disposition." With the world around I lived in, She would tell me, "B, be mindful and beware for men and children see . . . the life you lead may be the only bible some will ever read." I never really understood what that meant until I got older and met other people whose lives were like living bibles to me. They practiced a lot of the teachings I was taught as a child in church. Simple and commonly taught messages and life lessons, rarely practiced lessons. ; do unto to others . . . share the word of God . . . fast and pray were just to name a few. What she wanted me to understand was that even when you think someone is not paying you any attention, someone is reading the minutes of your life's story and watching your every move. It could be a child watching the clothes you select at Dillard's or the clerk who checked you out at the neighborhood H.E.B grocery store.

We constantly observe people and the things that they do, we make judgment calls even when we do not know their entire story.

In Shakespeare's Macbeth, he explains in the end, or it is in my interpretation that life is short, "a poor player that struts and frets his hour upon the stage and is heard no more . . . it is a tale . . . full of sound and fury . . . signifying nothing." I think that he only meant it signified nothing if no one ever knew you ever existed or knew your story.

All people matter, whether it is President Obama or the beggar under 45 North at Greenspoint trying to wipe your windshield with his filthy stolen squeegee only for you to ignore him . . . he still matters.

My mother Adelia has a story of her own after being married a few times. She survived a sort of apathetic husband, Craig. Craig told his other ex-wives that Adelia had cheated on him. It took thirty years after their divorce for the other wives to discover Craig had a set of twin daughters only two years younger than me and they were not divorced until I was seven years old. When Craig received a lot of his retirement money, all of his other wives except Adelia got a check for over fifty thousand dollars. Craig paid Adelia a total of 48 dollars in child support in 1977. Craig did have his high lights, for example he was very intelligent as far as education. He was a geologist for the oil company in Texas for over twenty-five years. He was really great with managing money and he loved gospel music. He had a really sensitive side he never liked to show and he was loved by me more than he would ever know and to me always more than he deserved if love were earned. I still wish he would have found a way to spend more time with me as a child than he did. I think sometimes the love of a child can change the way you see things. I was really surprised to learn he was a disc jockey when he was younger and called himself the Shadow. I used to imagine

Craig as some aspiring Tom Joyner who really had the potential, but never got the shot or opportunity to strut his stuff.

Adelia survived a giant of another husband, Perry Earl, who fell from grace when his boss sold his company instead of making Perry partner like he had promised Perry for years. Perry was a proud man with big dreams of owning his own White's store to leave to his son one day. I look at how she survived his depression and his insanity. Perry was so distraught at his surprising fate he resorted to drug use, physical abuse and finally suffered a massive stroke that caused his death at only fifty-five years old. He left ten surviving siblings and countless nieces and nephews behind. The worst thing he did was leave his youngest daughters without the great memories of him that I had, and he was not even my real father.

In the beginning, Perry adored Adelia, worshipped her and provided for her like no other man ever could a wife. Adelia loved him and for once in her life was *in* love with her husband. How devastating it was for Adelia to think she had been rescued, was finally in a safe and trusting relationship that would last forever only to have to watch her hero, her giant, her larger than life love fall from glory with his family, lose his integrity with the community and then die.

I watched her stand still in her front yard, after the funeral services of her husband, Edward, while the rest of the world moved around her. She stood there in the front yard looking out into the street at nothing. I imagine she was thinking of all the loss and all the devastation . . . just thinking, "Well Lord, I have lost my father, my mother, my brother, my only aunt on my father's side, my only aunt and uncle on my mother's side, I have lost my house trying to keep the home my mother and father built with their own hands, I have lost and lost and lost. What on earth do you want from me now?" Who will tell *her* story? Who will tell the story of such losses, such sorrows and what may have felt to her like spiritual homicide. Poor Adelia, who had played piano for the Lord since she was nine years old, had suffered so much. She started at Independence Baptist church on Holman St fifty years ago. Surely she must have thought The Lord was literally allowing or permitting her spirit to be killed a little every time someone was taken away at every loss . . . it killed her. Serving the Lord faithfully, never missing an opportunity to serve and this is the result, the ending of a faithful servant? She even played piano for Craig's father's funeral just hours after finding her own husband Edward dead in the home where they lived. Adelia still played piano for Craig's father because she felt it was the right thing to do.

I still look back on those days behind razor wired walls and tall guarded towers, and cry over the lessons I learned and things I never realized until I was there or until I left. According to Fast Facts online, there are over 89,000 non-violent offenders—non-violent people—in prison. There are almost three quarters of a million total inmates under Texas supervision. A person under supervision means they are either on probation—those who have committed crimes for the first time and more than likely have not gone to prison or they are on parole, those are the people who have been to prison and they will complete the rest of their time in the free world as opposed to behind bars. Either way, both parties will be subjected to perform and or participate in whatever their supervising state officer tells them to do. Some of the things one will do at any given time of request by their supervising officer are a urine analysis (UA). Others may be subjected to participate in some community service, 12 step program, AA/NA or alcoholics anonymous/narcotics anonymous. I remember the first UA I had. I was at the office on 34th near Mangum on the northwest side of Houston. I had a female probation officer. She wanted to stay in the bathroom with me and watch me pull my underwear down and pee. When I had other officers who would just send me in and out the restroom, I wondered was she just weird or had she had some bad experience with someone and she started watching everyone pee.

Your life is no longer your own simply because you are out of prison and on parole or probation. You are subject to random visits at home, inconvenient random visits on your new job with all of your coworkers looking on. You will be told to bring in check stubs every month or week whenever you come in as proof you are still working on the job they just came by to see you working on last week. You will be subjected to visit your probation or parole officer at his or her convenience, even if it means you may have to miss work to do whatever is expected whenever it is expected.

I recall an appointment where I was visited at work on Tuesday by my officer and I had an appointment on Thursday of the same week. I arrived at 4:00pm. I of course had to take off early for this. My appointment was for 4:30pm. I sat there in the lobby until 8:10pm before she came out, asked for my check stub and yes this was the same officer who had been to my job two days before. Then when she got the check stub, after I had been there waiting all that time, she gave me a card for my next appointment which was of course in the middle of the work week and in ten minutes after seeing her, it was time to go home.

You better not miss a single appointment or any of these stipulations in accordance with payments every month and fees. Missing a visit or not paying fees could be a direct violation causing immediate incarceration.

The system is designed for punishment and correction, not for the convenience of those who have broken the law. It is designed in such a way that your antisocial behavior is arrested. It is not to be comfortable and is certainly not a right to have probation or parole, it is a privilege granted by a judge. If you are serious about regaining your integrity, maintaining your freedom, rebuilding trusting relationships with your community, this is no problem . . . not an inconvenience at all. For the others, prison becomes a revolving door. There are those who will just not get it that they have forfeited their opportunity for freedom. The rights that come with freedom, such as living wherever you want to live without having to report it to anyone, that option is no longer available. Some people get stuck doing the same old thing or same old crime getting the same old results, thinking this time they won't get caught . . . Sound familiar?

I was one of those numbers, a statistic, and I believe it is high time to give the world a different view of events of what happens behind bars. After all, people in prison are just that—people. It doesn't matter how they got behind bars, they were born; they hurt, they cry, they bleed, and they will still die like everyone else.

You could start my story a lot of different places on my life's timeline, but I will start with when I was arrested while on my job. in August, 1994. I had a great job. I worked 10am till 6pm. I lived fifteen minutes from Dairy Ashford where my job was located. I was good at my job too. Being a lesbian, I loved working around all of the beautiful women. For some reason the ratio of women tomen in most office workplaces are 6 to1and why is it the male is usually the supervisor.

I always had a longing to be rich and never could figure out how to be rich overnight. I would save stocks and buy, but eventually would cash them out whenever a family crisis would happen. I was in the 401k program but I never could save more than what I earned in a year . . . it just never occurred to me that these things take time. I always felt like I was running out of time,

I wanted to be rich and when I would look at the literally millions I would bring in to the company and I was not even making a tenth of the earnings I brought in, I somehow felt cheated. I felt like someone owed me something. I looked at how a lot of fathers would not pay child support for one child, but would for other children who were succeeding. I wanted to have a better chance. I was dark skinned, bigger than most could appreciate and constantly over looked because I was darker and bigger. I wanted everything I saw Jasmine Guy, Pebbles and Vanessa Williams having in the 80's. I wanted the world to see me and love me.

A woman, I will call M., was seven years older than me. Her hair was in a braided up do away from her face. She was 5'5", gorgeous caramel colored skin, large round eyes and beautiful teeth. M. may have weighed 120-130 pounds realistically. I am sure she wore a size 9/10 maybe even some 8's depending on the store. Her hands and feet were slender compared to most women I knew. She wore a size 8 in shoes. Her fingers were slender with no scars or huge veins that would to me make then a little less attractive.

She always wore a suit and had neatly manicured hands and feet. She had two daughters. M. was recently divorced and seemed to have a sarcastic since of humor, which was attractive to me as well. She did not hang out with any of the clicks of older women. She was exciting to me, something different. So when she showed a little interest, I showed it back in return.

We took drives to Galveston on the weekends sometimes. We would dream of owning one those huge beach houses west of the seawall just before San Luis Pass. We would go to the carnivals or we would just hang out at her town home off Sandpiper on the southwest side whenever her ex husband had the girls.

We would drink amaretto sours, listen to music and talk. She had an atrium in the middle of the house she had filled with beautiful exotic and colorful plants. She later filled it with koi fish the last time I was there.

We never talked about anything intimate or too personal, but I felt a sincere closeness with her I had never felt with any other female. She was not like a sister, or even like any family, she was simply a beautiful woman who did not care about my sexual orientation. She once took her top off in front of me when I was waiting on her to change clothes when we were going to the movies. "I know you have seen breasts before B, don't act like that with me." She said teasingly.

"I have seen plenty of breasts just not yours . . . don't you act like that with me . . . hahahahaha" I told her in return. "Oh B, you would not touch me if I begged you, you are too scared. I know I see that fear in your eyes." She told me laughing and pointing her finger at me. I never took any of her flirts seriously, She was not bisexual to me and I would not have destroyed what I felt we had, just to have sex with her.

"Trust me, if you have never been there with a female don't let me be your first." I am not good with amateurs." I said. She knew I was attracted to her like a moth to a flame. I remember it like it was yesterday. She teased a lot, but we never messed around.

Everything she told me, I believed. We talked about getting rich off the company, but I did not think she was serious. I worked in the rebate department for toll free numbers. When companies have toll free numbers and called into me every month, I had the power to refund them for calls made to their toll free numbers that were under thirty seconds. The company would refund the calls because any real business took longer than thirty seconds and if the calls were less than that, it was presumed the calls were probably dialed in error and the companies would be reimbursed for whatever amount they paid on the previous month's bills for those calls.

M. thought it would work if we set up a fake account under her boyfriend's computer repair business name and send his company business refunds, that of course were not for real calls thirty seconds or otherwise.

I trusted her idea for several reasons, she had worked there longer than I had, she said she had done this before and I was infatuated with this older woman who could have told me I could fall on a sword and I would not die and I would have believed her. M was beautiful to me. I was attracted to how professional she always looked, spoke and carried herself. M. had her boyfriend set up a toll free number with his computer repair business. The refund checks were to go to his PO Box on SanFelipe. I never told a soul until after three months of these checks I had issued and no money had funneled down to me.

I only trusted my best friend Courntee and at that time my partner Telise. Courtnee could not believe that I trusted M to give me my thirty percent of all of these checks. Courtnee made me realize the fool I was putting my code in the computer funneling these fake checks, putting my job and freedom at risk for a thirty percent cut when I was doing eighty percent of the work. When June came, that made four months and I still had not seen a dime. I had issued over fifty thousand dollars in checks and still had not seen a dime. I decided that I was going to set up my own dummy accounts and have checks sent to where I could control the money. M. kept telling me that the checks must have been lost in the mail. I no longer believed her. I did not know if she was lying to me or if she was telling me the lie her Nigerian boyfriend was telling her, either way my panic level was through the roof. I had to come up with plan B and I had to do it fast because I knew my time was running out. I knew it would only be a matter of days before I was caught and I knew since I was already on probation for a gun charge from '91 and a forgery charge from '91 that catching a new case or new cases would definitely send my ass straight to prison.

I looked on the accounts as deep as I could go with her boyfriend's business and discovered that corporate security had been looking at the accounts, so had M's other boyfriend been looking at the accounts, whom I later discovered worked for corporate security. There were codes for each employee and those codes were recorded on the history of the computer log. You just had to know where to look.

I panicked and started to think of what I needed to do. I needed to steal as much money as I could because I was definitely going to jail. I did not want to go without an effort of trying to get something out of the deal. I talked to Cedric my brother's best friend and Perry Jr., my little brother and told them what my plan was. I would set up a fake account and have the checks sent to a p.o. box. We would split everything 50/50, but I needed to move fast because I was sure it would only be a matter of time before the police would arrest me. My plan was to collect a quarter of a million and stash it or bury it until I got out of prison. I was sure that I would not be there forever.

I assured Cedric, my brother's best friend who was like a little brother to me too, and Jr. that nothing would happen to them. The story would be that I had 401k money, lost my ID and they were helping me out by having the checks sent to them. They were still in high school, had never been arrested and I would do everything in my power to make sure they would not be in trouble. Being a somewhat habitual offender and bender of the law, I knew for them the worse case scenario meant probation for them. I figured worse case scenario, they could survive that. If they stuck to the story, they should be able to skate by the probation as well.

We hustled over fifty thousand in a month. I had Courtnee and my girl Telise in on the deal as well. I was stashing money in my apartment for when it all hit the fan. I trusted Telise to be by my side when it was all over and I would tell her where I hid the money after I was arrested and she and her two girls could live off that and keep the townhouse I bought for us on Wilcrest.

Needless to say, the plan did not work. M. turned me over to corporate who turned me over to the FBI. My mother, who was completely clueless to the entire thing, was harassed on her job with the IRS. They investigated her finances, which she had none. They questioned her neighbors and she was under investigation and interrogation worse on her job and I was the criminal.

I had written letters for Cedric and Perry that explained how sorry I was about lying to them. The letter stated the money was not 401k money and to please forgive me. They were supposed to use the letters as evidence against me and proof they had been fooled and were innocent. My mother was not buying the story. She drilled Perry asking more and more questions. Because he was afraid of her, he would sing like a canary to avoid getting beat to death by Adelia. I on the other hand, she would never get any information out of me. I had survived the beatings and was now untouchable to catch whippings, at least that is what she thought I thought. Truth is to this day I will not lie to my mother and had she asked me . . . I would have told her the truth. I am so glad she never asked me because I was also still afraid of catching a whipping at 27 years old.

"So Perry, you expect me to believe that B never told you the truth, you are completely innocent . . . you know nothing about this shit?" my mother would scold him with her head tilted and eyes squinted ending her question in falsetto.

"Uh . . . no ma'am, I didn't know anything. I was just trying to help her out." Perry would answer with the look of a scared two year old on his face.

"That's bullshit Perry, I cannot believe you are going to let your sister go to prison for something you are a part of and worse than that,

I cannot believe you are standing there lying to me and I have not knocked the hell out of you yet . . . tell the truth Perry . . . You tell the truth!" Adelia repeated as she swung at the 6foot 4 inch giant of a little brother. Needless to say in the end, she made my brother tell the police the truth, which in turn made Cedric tell the truth and they wound up in jail and finally on probation.

I was originally offered 25 years for each case; that amounted to 100 years . I was charged with computer fraud, mail fraud which was a federal offense, violation of probation and theft $100k-$200k.

I was brought into the conference room at work. There were four really angry looking white men. I had stolen good white people's money with my black ass and they were really pissed about it. They did not want the money back, they did not want to negotiate anything, and they wanted me in prison for life, like I was Andrea Yates or something. Fortunately for me, stealing the money the way I did, the maximum I could have gotten was 25 years for each case. The problem I faced was whether they would run the sentences concurrently also termed as "cc". This would mean if I got 25 years for each case, I would be doing the time for all four cases at the same time as opposed to stacked. Stacked would mean I would do 25 years for one crime first, then after I finished that time, I would do the time for the next crime and that would keep going until I practically died in prison for stealing money . . . not for killing my parents, not for killing my children, but for stealing money that would be replaced because it was in an FDIC bank where the checks were cashed. I probably would have killed myself if I would have gotten stacked, there was no way I would be able to do 100 years in my mind much less physically. Time is all in your mind anyway. No one ever says it, but we are all doing time. We are all just living on borrowed time until we die. Does not matter if you are living like the Kardashians or like the mentally ill homeless man with the prosthetic leg, we all just do our time living until we die all the same. I could not believe I would be doing more time than the money I tried to steal, which was more valuable?

I was only 27 years old and it looked like I would be spending the rest of my life in prison. The mystery was where all the money was. I laugh even to this day at that question because so many people thought I really had it all buried somewhere waiting until I was out of prison and off parole before I would dig it up and be rich. Everyone assumed I knew the statute of limitations, that I could not be charged again and if no one knew where it was but me, I would be going back to get it one day.

Where was the money? The answer really was quite simple—gone. It was all gone; all $233,169.53 is and was all gone. I paid $10k on the townhouse on Wilcrest. I paid $4k on getting Telisa's car repaired, I paid $4k on new furniture for my old apartment, and $4k on Telise's kids, I hid $5k in my apartment which I had planned on getting later, but later never came. I told everyone that I had hidden the money on the east side of the largest pine tree in my grandmother's yard. There is a huge knot on the tree, I buried it there. Needless to say, the tree was cut down and there was no money found, because there was no money . . . it was all gone.

I was okay with going to prison for a long time at first. I did not realize what I had gotten myself into and I was more concerned about my brothers and my family. I would have gladly taken 100 years, if that meant they would leave everyone else alone, but they did not. My mother was harassed for years on her job at the IRS, my brothers got probation for what seemed like forever and the disappointment the rest of my family had was enough to shame me into staying into prison forever anyway.

I had so many thoughts as to why I did it at first. I wanted to help my mother with my little brother and my little sister. She was a single parent and was always struggling; she had four jobs at this time and no car. I had a lot of anger towards my real father because I felt he never stepped up to at least help with the things I needed. Helping with the things I needed to help my mother with some of the finances. He made good money working for the oil companies as a geologist, testing rocks and soil for oil . . . I was his first born child and the last thing on his mind. I was angry I could not finish school at UT Austin because I had no money and my mother did not want me tied up in loans. I was angry that my hero, my stepfather Perry Earl Sr. who wanted nothing but the best for his family and he did the right things only for everything to turn out wrong. He had stopped providing for us and I was mad about that too. I was angry that he loved me so much and I resented that he was there when all of this was going on. He was too good to me and not my real father. I was angry that I learned to appreciate Perry Earl and eventually admired him for the amazing man he was and never had the courage to tell him.

I was angry at the millions I would make for the phone company selling toll free numbers to companies like Verizon, Houston Cellular and Smoke Signal home phone services while I watched my grandmother struggle to pay unexplained ridiculously high phone bills and people selling her tele-go phones that are now of course obsolete. Even the smallest of businesses made millions, literally millions and my mother was struggling with four jobs trying to keep the lights on. I had heard that crime did not pay, but I would have been glad for a loan or trade. I would have traded my life minutes for my mother to get some financial relief long before she dies, even if the cost was my life minutes being spent in jail. It was just money and I just wanted to get some of it, a lot of it to get a break. What was incredible to me is that if you embezzle money illegally without violence, money a company would never miss, the system wants you in prison for life, but if you are a Catholic priest, a nasty deacon, a college coach or a Baptist preacher who has fondled, sucked and fucked over little boys and practically ruined their entire life, you get notoriety via all the publicity on the news and in the papers and even book and movie deals while the victims contemplate suicide.

Detective Laboda seemed to like me or at least not hate me like the other good white people. He was the one who put the handcuffs on me in the elevator instead of in the conference room when he read me my rights. He was a US postal investigator. I rode in the back seat of his black jeep Cherokee from S. Dairy Ashford to 1301 Franklin St. Downtown Houston, Texas.

I was asked a million times the same hundred questions. It took 22 hours of questions from clerk to clerk and floor to floor before I was allowed to strip out of my regular clothes and into the Harris County oranges. I had to sleep on the floor before I was temporarily assigned to an underground room in a tunnel. I was all alone for what seemed like days. There were no windows, no lights, no beds, no chairs or benches just a drainage hole in the floor and glass windows on one side and a wall on the other. I was not afraid nor in shock of what was actually happening. I think this is what happens to a lot of criminals when you see them in court and they appear to have no remorse, I think it is because reality has not set in just yet.

Later on, I was to follow a deputy to another floor where there were other women. I spoke to no one, I said nothing and just went through motions trying to wrap my mind around the fact that I would not be leaving, I would not be seeing any of my family or associates again. I do not know why at the time that seemed important to me considering the reason I felt I was a good candidate for a life of crime was because I felt I would not be missed whenever I went to jail. I missed my mother from when I was a child. I missed how I felt she loved me and how as time passed and I got older, she began to hate what I was becoming.

I loved everything she hated. In elementary school, I was accepted to Betsy Ross' vanguard program and she sent me to Durkee. I wanted to go to Burbank middle school with my friends from Durkee and she sent me to Hamilton. I was accepted to H.S.P.V.A. and would have been one of the first graduating classes had I gone, she sent me to Waltrip. I wanted to go to T.S.U with my friends from Waltrip and she sent me to U.T. where I failed her like I had over and over and over again. She wanted me to be all feminine with make-up, dresses, heels and jewels. I wanted to wear jeans, plaid button down shirts and boots. It became too clear to me when I turned sixteen, that I would never be who she wanted me to be or I would never be me if I was.

Strangest thing is that I thought of all the places I had been, the times I had long before sitting on the concrete floors of the county jail. I thought about club Uptown/Downtown, how me and my small circle of queer friends would have a blast. I thought about the days of the juke joint Jacks on the corner of Leeland and Caroline and all of the queens who are long gone or no longer the celebrities they appeared to be to me then.

I thought of how I had asked Precious a good friend of mine, to marry me and he married Dee instead. No I am not still bitter about it. I thought about how Cherry and I, another good friend, had gotten drunk together in Galveston and peed on the jetty under the moon and laughed about it. I thought about how we went to sleep at my grandmother's house on the floor because it was the closest place, we couldn't make it home from being so tired and drunk. I thought of people and faces and places I knew I would never see again. I still did not feel anything that felt like remorse for what I had done, only loss for myself and regret for getting my family involved. I did not feel sorrow, nor regret except for the fact that I had tangled my brothers in this shit. I did not feel like I had wasted my life. I honestly felt like

I had lived all I had to live. I was actually ready to die . . . maybe that was why I had thrown away all of my dreams and education, I felt like I had lost so many things till nothing mattered not even me. My dreams of being an actress, a writer, even finishing college all shot and deferred because I did not have enough financial support and guidance with my mother alone. I did not have anyone encouraging me to be me. I was encouraged NOT to be me.

I only knew how to be the me that came natural. I would have been content I guess with becoming whomever Adelia wanted me to be except I did not know how. Being a frilly all feminine girl to me was like being tossed in Germany and people talking to me in german, making gestures as to what they wanted me to do. I simply did not get it the concept or even the importance of being this other person. I felt comfortable with me and liked me, but the people I loved did not. I had a hard enough time with the comments people made on the job, in clothing stores, at the church, pretty much anywhere there were people not like me.

I was encouraged not to wear clothes that were comfortable, but clothes that made me look more lady like. I was discouraged not to attend HSPVA when they opened the school here in Houston because Adelia said there were too many fags and bulldaggas there. I was encouraged to attend church religiously although the girls at church my age, were all having sex and tried to have me set up for a sexual encounter with a boy five years older than me. I was discouraged to write the stories I loved writing so much. I was taught how ladies stand, sit, eat and walked. I was supposed to yes ma'am every old lady who talked about my mother behind her back at church. I was to yes sir every old perverted deacon who tried to feel my breasts or get me to go off with them quietly in some other part of the church. I was not to wear pants, like men or cut my hair. I was to marry a man, have children and work in the church until I died. I was to work in the same church that housed and welcomed all these child predators, thieves and money changers, back biting, hypocrites who could care less about the true spiritual growth of any member of the church.

We belonged to some church my whole life and yet not one pastor bothered to pray for my mother or visit her when I was in prison. Not one pastor nor church family member reached out to my mother one time to offer even moral support when she was battling ovarian cancer. Church . . . family . . . I was fine with the church not caring about my lost sheep ass, I never wanted to be in their buildings anyway, but my mother was good to those people and for her to have struggled and worked like she did, I do not see how any of those people could call themselves Christians and not see about my mother, for this I could not feel remorse for trying something else to make a better life for her and my family.

There is a passage in the bible I finally sent to Craig, my natural father, when I finally did write him. Matthew 25:41-46 "Then shall he say also unto them on the left hand, Depart from me, ye cursed, into everlasting fire, prepared for the devil and his angels: For I was an hungered, and ye gave me no meat: I was thirsty, and ye gave me no drunk: I was a stranger, and ye took me not in: naked, and ye clothed me not: sick, and in prison, and ye visited me not." All of the church sermons I had heard my whole life, no one ever preached on this one. From Star Bethel Baptist where I was baptized to New Hope where all my hopes died along with the church. This was the common behavior I was used to from Christians . . . and here I was not realizing I felt my natural father had treated his child the same way.

When my mother had those four jobs, we ate wieners and bread mostly. I would ask Craig to help and not once would he, because I had a little brother and sister who were not his children. His logic was, how could he bring something to eat for just me? He made it clear he would not do anything for Perry Sr.'s children although Perry had raised his child. He would tell me if my mother had not asked him for help that meant I must not have needed it. I asked him to buy my school clothes to preserve the money I earned from Tempo fashions, the clothing store where I worked. The money my mother would put with mine would be for the little kids school clothes. He would ask, "don't you have a job?" And now here I was in prison, he never once came to see me in the county, not once did he come to see me. I was not certain that I did not want to be nor have anything to do with the Christians I had known my whole life. I knew I had no family except my mother, my brothers and my little sister. I knew that one day I would be back in the free world and when I did, I would have a different view of people altogether, I would spend a lot of time redefining what Christian meant to me.

I spent a lot of time thinking about the men in my life. There weren't too many good pictures. I had men in my life who abandoned their children, who could not handle defeat, men who did not care about people, preachers and church men who constantly had sex on their minds, men who cheated women out their money, who beat women, who raped children; these were the men I knew of and about. I wanted to be better than a man. I wanted to be more than a woman. I would not surrender to defeat, I would get back up the next day and fight again. I would defend and love children like my mama did me. I would provide for my little brother and sister some kind of way without the help of a man. I would be stronger, wiser and live longer than any of the men I knew and had known.

I wanted something different with the Lord. I did not know what it would be, but I knew I was not going to just attend church religiously with the same people who preached I was going to hell for being who and what I was born as, while pastors were on the news for sexting young men. The first thing out of all the Christian's mouths about that was, "he is just a man, people need to quit putting pastors on a pedestal, they make mistakes like anyone else."

I was going to hell for sleeping with women, but the leaders were going to heaven for having children outside their marriage, for being accused of child molestation, for being accused of beating their wives, for being accused of misappropriation of church funds? This made no sense to me at all. What did make sense was that I was happier around people who did not judge me. People who loved me just like they saw me and was not trying to change a thing about me. I wanted to find that kind of relationship with the Lord, where no matter what, He still loved me. I was so confused with the messages I was taught. One Sunday I was going to hell and the next Sunday God loved me unconditionally . . . I choose the latter to believe.

I had to get a job at fifteen at a clothing store called Tempo Fashions where my mother worked just to keep the lights on in our two bedroom townhouse. The first address we had after my mother left Perry Earl Sr. was off Antoine. When we moved there, there were no counseling sessions, no conversations about what was going on with my father and Adelia, nor about the fact that the life and home we were used to was gone. I changed a lot then because of this separation of my parents causing this new life I had to adjust to. I had more responsibility. I had siblings who had become like my children now. Thoughts about bills and stuff we needed were my new priorities instead of whether I could walk around the neighborhood with David, Laurice, and Trent. I had bills to pay and school grades to keep up. I had children to make sure they got baths and were fed if my mother did not make it home in time for these things to happen. Adelia was literally hitch hiking from one job to another. Sometimes she barely made it in only to turn around and go out to another job. I became numb to what I wanted, what I dreamed seemed to not matter anymore. I did not care any more about dating, the parties schoolmates were having, it was not like I could ever go. I felt like all that mattered was the acquisition of stuff I hoped I would not lose again. I lost my gold cross earrings my mother struggled to buy somewhere in the move, I bought some fake ones in their place. I lost my favorite pair of Fila tennis shoes I had waited and waited for, I bought a pair of Pro-wings in their place. All I kept trying to do was keep who I had and what I had. I had David as my best friend; he would only become Courtnee, but would never leave me like the stuff did.

I was assigned to B-3; that was my tank. The tanks were identified by letters and numbers. They are the actual jail cells where the inmates reside, while I was there, I saw how people left lockup, came back and left again. It was a revolving door. Some women came in lying to themselves and others about how they were going to change their lives, blah, blah, blah and as soon as they were released, the next weekend they would come back, wearing their orange outfits that didn't fit, and dragging their blue mat into my tank. One white woman, Susan, told me she had given birth to nine children, because even though she was a prostitute, she did not believe in abortion—like that made sense. The killing part about her story is that none of them were living with her and all of their fathers were black.

Drug addicted inmates were something totally different. They came in with diseases and unbelievable odors. A lot of them would be picking at their skin, or their hair was plucked out or some other part of their body was scarred with self-inflicted damages.

I watched a crack head's water break and she was so screwed up, she didn't even know she was about to have a baby. I witnessed a lot of weird things and was exposed to a whole nother life I had not been introduced to before, in spite of my exciting rough life I had created with theft via checks. There was a woman whose entire top of her head had been plucked clean. She said it was because some cop she was screwing had pulled her by her hair and dumped her in the dumpster. He pulled all of her hair out. The real story was that some people pull out their hair or pick at their skin or smack a lot when they are on crack. Some people pop their lips a lot like they are eating really sticky peanut butter. One time, I felt a needle in a girl's vagina. She had broken it off right in her pelvic bone area trying to get rid of the needle because the cops were coming. The stories of crack just never seemed to end. I only felt her vagina to feel the needle. I thought it was really interesting. She was exhibiting the area like she was taking money for shows. I would sometimes watch her sway back and forth appearing to be sleepy. I was later informed that she was not on crack, she was on heroin. The information these women told me I kept in my memory bank. I thought of one day telling their stories, but the stories of hookers and hoes had already been told in several ways with the film "Pimps up/Hoes down."

There was a girl named Sabrah who came through the county while I was there. She was really pretty and had the story that she inherited thirty thousand dollars and smoked it all up in thirty days. She explained how she was now homeless, without family and living from place to place. I believed her. She talked about how her dad died and left her the money. How her mother did not even know she would get that much or else she would have tried to stop her from getting the money, Sabrah said jokingly. How she wished her mother would have known a lot of things. She claimed he only left her the money to make up for molesting her when she was a child. She said it like it was nothing, without showing any hurt. I guess after so much crack and so much time passed, it doesn't even bother you to talk about it if you talk about it enough.

I spent six months in Harris County. Tommy Thomas as sherriff. You would have never guessed I had won the Optimist oratorical contest in 1983 and was even in the newspaper. You would have never guessed that I had won the speech contest and beat out the infamous Marcus Brown at UT in 1989. No one would have ever suspected me of being a member of the National honor society, Quill and Scroll and French National honor society. I would have never been mistaken as the girl who graduated from the international baccalaureate program in the top ten percent of my class of 368 as I played cards with Kotex boxes and rigged a television with Kotex tape. I played dominoes with carved blue soap. I slept with at least four different women and didn't care about anything or anyone. It did not even matter that my chances of getting AIDS were definitely increased, considering the selection of prostitutes and other fast women who were in there with me.

But everything wasn't fun and games. I ate cold soups and took cold meds so I could sleep. I refused to eat most of the food they served in jail because I once found a fat grub worm that appeared to be getting fatter off the stuff on the tray they delivered to me. I just bought stuff off commissary with the little money I had.

Time in the County is easy for people who do not scare easily. You get visits and you get to use the phone. You can still act like a selfish idiot and call people all day and night with their phones being charged fees to talk to you, not caring that their lives have not stopped just because yours has. All you think about is what you want and what you need—from soap and deodorant to freedom.

The guards usually disappeared after doing a head count and feeding time. The county guards were the only free world people I would see regularly and I did not see them except at count time or feeding time. Most of them avoided us, we were now animals to them in a cage I guess. I can only remember two of them. Mr. Sam was a nice, tall black man who would give the girls Tylenol if they were in pain. He paid more attention to what was going on than the rest. For some reason, I looked forward to seeing him whenever he worked. His kindness reminded me that there was another world out there and B3 was not all there was. I think I had started doubting if I had ever really been free, I had been locked up in the same room for six months without any daylight, fresh air or real food. So seeing someone who smelled like something other than jail, looked like a real person and not a crack head, brought back memories or what I thought was memories.

The other guard was a really handsome white man who could sing country like nobody's business. I wasn't a big fan of country music at the time, but I recognized a great voice and he definitely had one He was kind too. He would give us extra soap and the baking soda packets. The soda packets were used for a lot of things, you brushed your teeth, used it as deodorant and you could clean with it. It was simply baking soda with a touch of mint. Other than those two, for six months day in and day out, it was surreal. Count time, breakfast, count time . . . lunch . . . count time dinner . . . every single day.

Six months in the county and I never had a fight. I did have to threaten this woman named Marquette . Marquette claimed she was a school bus driver for Kashmere high school. Claimed she was only in there for traffic tickets. She was sleeping on three mats and a homeless white woman came in without a mat at all. The white woman was sleeping on the cold ass floor in the dead of winter—and those fools had the air conditioner on.

The guard had came in and told Marquette to unass one of the blankets and one of the mats or he would come in and take everyone's blankets and mats because we all were supposed to only have one blanket and only one mat. It made no sense for all of us to lose what little we had because she wanted to be greedy. Made no sense that she saw this woman shivering on the floor, cold and hungry and she still did not unass the mat and blanket. I had to threaten Marquette to make her give up one of those county mats to the woman. "yeah bitch I'm gone shut my eyes and when I wake up that crack head on the floor better have a damn mat and blanket before the guards come or else I am gona beat your ass. You know what kind of time I got, you seen my damn court papers so I ain't got shit to lose bitch but this got damn blanket and mat and I will be damned if you or nary bitch in here make me lose the shit I got when y'all bitch asses is going home to real shit." It took a while before she took my threats serious, but I meant it. I had put a can of sardines in my sock and I was going to bust that bitch across her head until my mind changed as my mama used to say. "Close your eyes Marquette without unassing that damn mat and blanket and I bet you your ass won't wake up . . . I ain't got shit to lose, I got a fucking 100 years . . . you got time like that?" She was scared to move while I threatened her. I used the oldest threat in the book, no I was not going anywhere any time soon, yes I would have beaten the shit out of her with that can of sardines if I would have lost my shit and had to sleep in the cold without a blanket or mat when her ass was going home soon, but no . . . I would not have been able to make her stay there because she got into a fight in the county. Only in real TDCJ prison would fights really matter, but she did not know that and was not about to find out. She finally gave her one of those mats and a blanket.

I was a force to be dealt with in County. Everyone was aware that I was not going home any time soon. Everyone knew that I was definitely going to prison, so people did not fuck with me and I could do whatever I wanted. When I found out Telise had been arrested and was on the same floor as me, I sent her a kite. A kite was basically a letter sent by someone who channeled it somehow to the person intended for a small fee, like a ramen noodle soup or stamps I knew the ins and outs of everything. I knew how to hustle needle and thread in to sew up those God awful uniforms that never covered my chest properly. I was still a female and did not like exposing my breasts and the cut on those uniforms were for men, not women with breasts. I sewed up the pants which were bell bottomed, not my style at the time. I hustled good food from the kitchen and bleach to clean the showers and real bar soap without having to buy it from commissary. I knew how to hustle extra fruit and hair braids from women who had studs for lovers without the studs getting all upset about their girl's hands all over my head. I knew how to get messages to people in the free world and because of my crazy behavior prior to jail, they believed any threats I made, being in the county definitely increased my street credits even if I was not even trying to get them. . Most of my life, I was raised solely by my mother, Adelia. She was the only person on earth I feared. Any woman who can give birth to three children, work three to four jobs at one time, have three husbands and out live them all, bury her father, uncle, aunts, brother, find one husband dead, survive cancer twice, bleed seven days and still not die, was to be feared. She could whoop you like you killed someone and she would also defend you like she was Jesus' personal assistant. Yeah, that Adelia was to be feared, but she was the only one I feared.

After I had been there for six months, it was the natural assumption I would be pulling chain. Pulling chain meant that you would leave for a real prison unit soon. Little did I know that one Monday morning, around midnight, I would be shackled from my waist to my wrists and then attached to someone else.

We were stuck in a holding cell where we laid on the floor like dogs until the bus came. It was day light when we left. The Blue Bird bus had these silver plates over the windows with slits just enough to let some light in. The seats were hard plastic. All the way in the back was a man in a gray uniform with a shotgun. Two more gray-uniformed people were in the front.

I sat next to the window wondering, *what is going to happen to me now?* The County had been so predictable and now I was leaving and did not even know where I was going. That is where the real story began.

DAYTON, TEXAS

We were unloaded at a place covered with gray and blue tin buildings. There was land everywhere, covered with green grass and populated with horses. I could not believe the horses. I had never seen any close up.

There were people in gray clothes and cowboy has walking about, now that was a joke to me. There is a general perception that if you are from Texas, you are familiar with cowboy hats and livestock. The truth of the matter is *that* could not be further from the actual truth.

They marched us to what looked like a garage and issued each of us a set of clothes—a white gown, a pair of gray socks, and a pair of boots. They stood us in a hallway and we were told to take icy cold showers for about two minutes. I did the best I could. They issued me a pair of white panties because at the county I wore colorful drawers and they do not allow those in prison. They made me take my hazel contacts out of my eyes and flush them down the toilet. That was a big problem for me because they were prescribed. They also issued me a white bra.

After we got dressed, they led us in a line to the inside of the unit. It was a chow line. We ate a piece of link sausage, green beans, and pears and we drank a cup of water. The food was better than in the County. It was a big step up.

Then, we went to another line where we were issued a pair of white pants and a white shirt. It was cold when we arrived but we were not issued the state jackets for two more weeks. Finally, we were led to the K-dorm, a temporary dormitory for those who had not been classified just yet.

K-dorm was a garage with extremely high ceilings. Voices echoed everywhere. We were upstairs and slept in bunks. There were gates like those in the County; they were opened with buttons operated from the "picket," temporary offices for the guards on duty for the dorms.

There were outside pickets and inside pickets. The outside pickets were about two stories high and usually housed a guard who could shoot the wings off a hummingbird.

We never left the dorm except for chow and showers. Showers were humiliating. There were no doors or curtains on them and the opening faced the picket. Sometimes men ran the picket. I immediately felt like my rights were being violated.

About two weeks later, I was placed in new temporary housing, D-3-21. I was issued a state ID card, which had my picture and my number, 807513. My name is Brandy Denise Anderson, but from that day on I would be known as 807513. We were told our ID must be on us at all times or that would be a case. A case was basically a disciplinary write up and after so many, the parole board would give you a set off, meaning if you were to see them soon, they would send you written notification that they were setting off the time you were to be seen originally to a later date. That later date could be anywhere from six months to a few years. It was quickly brought to my attention that everything was a case. Talking, walking, breathing, even farting could get you a case if you did not get permission to do it.

I was no longer a human being, I was an inmate. I would be told when I could shower, when I could eat, what I could eat and where I could go, when I could go and when I could speak to another inmate. Violation of any of those rules could result in a case.

My bunk was on top. I was not afraid, even though the women in that tank were pretty darn scary looking. Mama Grace was the scariest. She was short and stocky with thick gray wiry hair and thick glasses. She had a deep raspy voice and was allegedly there for murder. Everyone, and I do mean *everyone* else, was there for drugs. They either tried to use it, sell it, buy it, move it, deliver it or manufacture it.

It wasn't long before I wrote my mama and started begging for stuff. I begged for money, books, and visits. I never once wrote to ask how she was doing. I was selfish and all that mattered was how I was and what I thought I needed. Adelia did the best she could. She sent money and letters and she came to visit me every single Sunday after she was done playing piano for the church.

I look back on those days and I have such regret for all that I put her through. She never deserved that. She was in prison with me. I never did that time alone, although I thought I did. I never considered for a moment that I was where I was supposed to be and it was not supposed to be comfortable or convenient.

When Adelia found out that I had no corrective lenses, she mailed them to the warden and demanded that I have them because I was close to being legally blind. I got the glasses and was placed on the hoe squad for my job.

Everyone had a job, or they went to school, Alcohol Anonymous (AA), or Rec, which was on a 20 x 30 concrete covered pad in the back of the dorm. No one was really busy, but they would do anything to get out of the dorm.

I was required to go to AA. I was not in there for drugs. I had never used drugs and I wasn't even a heavy drinker. I watched with great disgust the films where I watched people smoking crack. I watched the films of prostitutes trying to change their lives. I felt like I was being introduced to even more crime. I had never tried any drug of any kind at that time and had no intentions of it. When I would watch the films and listen to how euphoric the minds of the drug users were or how uninhibited the prostitutes felt not to mention the money they made . . . I wondered if I had the guts to do those things. I never had a yearning desire to be intimate with men and never thought about smoking crack, but when I was constantly mentally fed this stuff, I had to admit they now crossed my mind.

If you had any kind of communication with the guards, you had to fill out a form called an I-60. It was the form you sent if you needed to go to the doctor, to the infirmary, or anywhere that caused you to leave the dorm. Then they would send you a notice called a lay-in to take care of whatever you asked for via I-60, basically giving you a written permission slip.

I wrote the warden and told her that I felt I had been misclassified. I was in the dorm with a bunch of hookers and drug addicts. I was on the hoe squad, which only worked about four hours a day, and all I had was a few felonies for bad checks. She did not respond. In fact, it was rumored that all of the guards had a good laugh because I did not get the idea that inmates were equal . . . all offenders were offenders. All sin was sin.

I was thinking of writing a story about this one inmate Nita. Nita was a legend in her own time. She had gained notoriety in the free world because she looked just like a six foot two, hundred and fifty pound man. She had huge hands, a deep voice, chiseled face and gold teeth. There was absolutely nothing feminine about Nita whatsoever. I asked to interview Nita to start my novel. I figured hey, I have nothing but time and this is the perfect person to talk to who has been around long enough to have some good stories.

Nita told me about the moving company she and her sons had. I was looking for her to be mean somehow and yet the more I talked to her, the more I realized she was just a person. She had no real interesting stories of drama to tell, she had not killed anyone. She had not beaten her lover causing her to be in jail. She had not been on some high speed police chase, she believed in Christ, read her bible, treated people the way she wanted to be treated and that was pretty much it. I don't think she ever saw my vision of making her immortal with words. I just felt like legends should be written about and from what even the queens had told me, she was definitely a legend.

All it took was for one jealous guard to see all of my writings and she confiscated everything. She told me I was inciting a riot. Told me I should not be idolizing anyone like that. This dumb ass told me she was going to keep it and if she found any kind of conspiracy to escape that would be a free world case. I could not believe it. I was like this bitch must be new because I just got here and adding time to what seemed to me like eternity any way was no big deal. I was mentally prepared to never leave prison and never see the free world again any damn way. I was more pissed at the thought of her taking my writings because I figured she would use it to write her own novel with my material. I eventually got over it, Nita eventually left the unit and things were back to usual.

The time passed slowly, so slowly I could no longer stay quiet. I was incredibly attracted to an inmate named Carmelia. She was a dark-skinned, big-boned female who slept on the bottom bunk under Lisa, a light-skinned gorgeous girl from Dallas. Carmelia went by the name of Cameo. She had absolutely no interest in me. She was sleeping with a girl named Black who was cheating on her all the time with a girl in the dorm where Black was housed . . . I never wanted to sleep with Cameo because I heard she was a prostitute in the free world, but her dark features and her bubbly personality were incredibly attractive. Interesting how after I had taken an HIV test when I arrived in Dayton, I became a little more selective with the women I chose to be involved with.

Lisa had interest in me only because she found out I had not been a drug user in the free world and I had a little money on my commissary. However, she was bossy and mean. I really liked her when she was funny, but she was usually mean. She blamed it on being half Jamaican. I blamed it on just her choice to be a bully.

Truthfully, I was not even trying to hook up with any of the women there because I figured it would turn into a long-term relationship, considering most of us would be there for more than a few months. I was under the impression I was in the real prison. I did not know that I was only supposed to be there a year and that it was a transfer facility. I wound up being there something like 22 months straight on the same bunk.

"What are you eating?" Lisa asked one day.

"Just a soup with cheese and fritos," I said.

"You know me and Chili broke up. Found out she was also with a girl in the dorm she slept in, and a girl in E-dorm who wanted to kick my ass but I told her I was not with her anymore. Hahahhahahahaha." Chili was from another dorm and, really, I felt like she was a mean broad who liked to act like a dude inside the walls and then she probably had several boyfriends outside the walls. To me she was like a down low brother, the ones who in prison get their dicks sucked and they bend over for their butts to be exercised and then when they get in the free world, they will swear they never had an encounter with another man.

"Well, I am eating this. If you want some, you are more than welcome to whatever I have." Lisa didn't say anything; she just started tasting the food.

I did not mind sharing with her because she always shared with me. She offered me things when I did not have anything, even when she and Chili were together. Lisa and I were real friends and eventually became friends in the free world. I never forgot though how she married the man she let steal my money. I blamed her as much as myself because I felt like she knew he would do it and if she could see back then he could not be trusted, why would she marry him later on in life when she got out? Basically, I really did have some money here and there in the free world. I had some bonds in my name I needed cashed and the money was to be split as a courtesy of him cashing the checks for me fifty-fifty . . . No w to me that seemed more than generous to give a total stranger fifty percent of what I had, just to perform one duty. She trusted her man, and I trusted her. Needless to say, that was the first sign of many that he did not even give a damn about her because he cashed the checks, over a thousand dollars which would have lasted me my entire stay and disappeared. He never wrote her, he never came to see her after that incident to my knowledge. We never spoke of it again until twelve years later. I hurt her feelings because she honestly did not think he would do that, but I felt better letting her know I thought she married a jerk.

We befriended a woman older than us named Jewya, who was also from Dallas. She talked on and on about her daughters, Talia and Natalia She started calling me her daughter and thought my hooking up with Lisa would be a good idea. Neither Lisa nor I were interested in a long-term relationship, but we were addicted to relationships and felt we needed one now. We became an item.

In the beginning, there was no kissing or touching, just walks around the Rec yard, sitting at the tables together and we talked a lot . . . She was gorgeous as hell—beautiful gold skin, copper colored eyes and long shiny dark brown hair; she was just not my type.

Telise was my partner from the world. She was the love of my life. She was dark-skinned, heavy-set and sexy. She too had incredibly long black hair, and it was all real. Telise was really great with turning a dime into a dollar. She dressed professional even when she did nothing around the house. She did not use me like others had, but I was never sure if she loved me. She cheated on me and I still didn't care; I just wanted to work things out. She left me though. She sold my car and my house and sent me one letter that had on the outside flap, "The chapter is closed, closed, closed." It was written on my stationary. To this day, I think of that blue stationary with the moon and stars on it and the sealed flap with the words "closed closed closed" on the outside. I think I still have it.

"B, come on and let's play dominoes. You need to get off that bunk today," Lisa insisted.

"No, guys, let's play chess," Jewya said.

"I don't know how to play chess," I told her "I barely know Jewya, my uncles James and John showed me a long time ago, but I don't remember."

"Then, I will show you." Jewya insisted

Jewya was upset because they took her ID at the picket in exchange for the game and then the game was missing parts and we could not play. She argued with them trying to get them to understand that she did not want to return the game; she only wished to have all the parts to play.

The guards on this unit had little understanding with regards to inmates. Some of them would curse inmates, yell at them and even call them names. One female guard was beaten to a pulp in a particular incident. Rumor is she told the inmate that she would whip her ass if she did not sit on her bunk until the guard's shift was over. The inmate told her she was not going to sit on her bunk all day and she wish she would try to whip her ass. The guard, who apparently was incredibly unprofessional, walked in the dorm and the inmate knocked her out in one punch. Unfortunately for the guard, there were several punches thereafter that busted her left eye out of the socket. There was blood stained all in the crevices of the cemented walls. There was still blood on the cement when I was finally housed there.

The guard was fed up with talking to Jewya about the pieces and sent other guards in to arrest her. They handcuffed her and walked her out, I never saw her again.

I had been there for almost 21 months and had not had sex with anyone. Lisa and I had not even kissed simply because she didn't want to. We played games and walked around the pavement at Rec.

We always talked about the free world. She would tell me how she had been to Houston, had a cousin in Houston and that her brother was in the Texas Youth Commission. She had three daughters who lived with her and another one who lived in Alabama.

We shared enough to decide neither would be a threat in the free world, so we decided to write and look each other up when we get out. I was almost convinced that I was not getting out until I got paroled. Unfortunately, I got a set off for a year. That's when they do not give you an answer exactly; they just tell you they will check back with you later.

One day, she said, "B, I really need to talk to you for real."

"Alright, what's the matter?" I asked.

"I really don't know how to say this. I just have been locked up a long time. Me and Chili really didn't do anything but kiss and, B, I have to admit that I . . . well, being surrounded by nothing but women, I have been a little excited. I just kind of need to release some stress, I guess that would be a better way of saying it."

"You want to do it?"

"Shut up!" she said turning red in the face. "But, yeah. I need you to meet me in the shower." Even as bossy as she was, I had absolutely no objection to her request.

"Lisa, wait. Have you ever done this before? I am asking because sometimes you could catch some feelings you ain't used to and wind up . . ."

"Aw, shut up! We talked about this already . . . I ain't gay . . . I am not a lesbian. I just . . . just shut up and come on . . . and to answer your question, no, I haven't ever and you should feel honored. You will be the first to deflower me," she laughed.

No lie, I was scared of getting caught. I kept reminding myself that I was set off for a year with parole and if I did get caught it would only be my first case. I was not about to pass up someone who was not a prostitute and not an ex-addict. She had been caught with her boyfriend's drugs in his car. She wasn't trying to sell drugs nor buy drugs . . . she was just trying to get to work.

"Don't play with me, B. I expect you in shower number two in 15 minutes. The guard on duty, I know her. She's going over to D-2 for at least 30 minutes to talk to Chili."

"Yes ma'am, I ain't got a problem with it."

We waited for the guard to dim the lights on half the dorm. She always did, thinking that it would calm everyone down. She would do this if the dorm was still noisy after ten at night and she would hope no one would bother her. She was right. Most of the women would just shower and go to bed. The picket boss was in another dorm. Lisa was in the shower with just her gown on. She had talked a big game but now she was scared, and I started to feel like it wasn't the best idea if she was going to be frightened.

"Come on and do this so I can get it over with! I don't want to change my mind about this again." she demanded, although she was chuckling. I figured she must have debated about this before. I just wondered why she picked me if she always seemed to be so mean to me . . . or at least really bossy.

I knelt down below her. I had lost 60 pounds since the County. Working on the hoe squad was more exercise than I was used from the free world . . . That is the only way we both fit in that shower. Still, it was roomier than most would think.

She raised her dress and I touched her between her legs with my fingers first and then my tongue. Five minutes later, Lisa was releasing her stress. I was choking because her love came down way too fast. She trembled and began to fall. I caught her just as the door flung open and the guard was walking up to the restroom area.

"I'm a need to see your ID. Oh, I'm a need to see your ID too. Y'all both just got a case." The guard said with such an attitude.

We handed over our IDs and she took them to the picket. Lisa and I were laughing at how she fell out of the shower. I was still tripping over how she made it rain on my face.

The guard brought our IDs back and told Lisa she was surprised at her.

"Well, hell, you just mad because Chili ain't doing you." Lisa said.

"For that you can stay on your bunk," the guard replied.

"Whatever!" Lisa said throwing her hand up in the air.

"Keep talking shit and you gone wind up with another case."

"I don't care. I got a date and I am still going home."

Lisa only had a seven-year sentence and had done almost four. It was her first time in prison. She was right; she would be going home in a few days. The guard did not know what to say. I was not giving her any lip considering I did not have a date and was not the type to give guards lip. I just gave up my ID and went to my bunk. Now usually when these types of events happened, one would think someone would be embarrassed because they were caught. I was not in the slightest. I was actually pretty proud that I discovered a something new to me about some women, the squirting thing. I think it turned me on and considered looking other women up in the free world who could do this whenever I got out. I had that experience on my mind all night.

Some of the guards threatened you with statements like, "How are going to explain to your folks that you can't have visitors because you got a sex case?"

They failed to realize we were in prison, so nothing could be worse than telling our folks we were behind bars. I came from the free world a lesbian, so it would have been a surprise to my mother that it took me that long to get a sex case. True it would have embarrassed her, but really what could be more humiliating than for your peers and coworkers and church members to ask you where is B and you have to come up with a reason why she was no longer there and was not dead. Eventually, my mother had changed churches and I was not even a person to be remembered. To them my mother only had two children. I had not been around Acres Homes for so long until even in the hood when my mother's neighbors would have small talk, they only knew of two children. I no longer existed in the free world, I was obsolete and so a sex case would be obsolete as well.

I was not to the point where I didn't care, just at the point where I was content with where I was. The work was not hard and the food was edible. My friend, Dawn, sent me updates on what was happening in the free world. My mother was faithful in coming to see me every single Sunday at 2pm and sending money. I needed to learn how to be grateful and I would be fine.

I went and sat on my bunk. A new person came in for the bunk below. Her name was Ariopajita Ibanez. She was a very attractive, heavy-set, light-skinned, long-haired woman with an accent. She said she was from Honduras. She and Ebony, who was from North Carolina, became really great friends.

Lisa left a week later. I was still waiting for a lay-in to go to court for the sex case. I made friends with Ibanez and Ebony and sometime in the middle of the night, like thieves, the guards took me.

"Anderson, pack your stuff; your leaving," a voice called out to me.

"Where am I going?" I wondered and asked because I had become so familiar with where I was, leaving had not entered my mind.

"You are just leaving this place, thank God!" an associate named Kay Kay Green. She was from third ward in Houston. She was very curvy, petite and did not bother anyone. She was really Lisa's friend, but I ran into her a few times in the free world at a place in third ward off Dowling called C. Phil's.

"Bye, B," Ibanez and Ebony said just above a whisper.

I packed my commissary bag with the books that Bernette from AT&T had sent me. I also packed my Bible, which at that time had not even been opened except to write someone's address and spin number or TDC number.

Now, I was headed to where they separate the women from the girls. I still was not afraid. I should have been.

DEVIL'S ISLAND

T hey never take you straight to Point B. The purpose of this is to confuse or catch anyone who might be following the bus to break anyone out. Everything is a secret and after seeing ConAir with Nicolas Cage, I was inclined to believe it was not a bad idea. I was taken with about 20 other ladies on the Blue Bird off to a men's unit in the middle of the night. The next morning we were loaded up with even more girls who were put on the bus with us.

"Yeah, Jay, we headed for Devil's Island!" one of the ladies said to another on the bus. I didn't know anyone and felt like a kid in a new school. I hated not knowing so many things. I didn't know where I was going, didn't know anyone on the bus, and didn't know even where I was, other than somewhere in Texas. I thought we were heading west and maybe a little north only because my mother had taught me that the sun rises in the east and sets in the west. It was morning I thought and the sun was sort of behind us so I assumed we were headed west.

No lie, I was scared this time as I listened to the things that white girl was saying about Devil's Island.

The bus pulled behind a huge 20-foot gate. There was razor wire all around the unit and all around the back gate. I could see a man in gray walking around the bus with a mirror attached to a stick where he could roll it under the bus; he was checking for drugs, weapons, and even people trying to escape.

The people and the atmosphere were not as "friendly" as the facility in Dayton. Everyone had a stern look on their face like they had something on their minds. The silence was eerie. There were inmates walking around, even some at this back gate, but they looked like ghosts or clones, just didn't look like any life was in them, just existing to do a job wherever they were placed.

We were put in a cage outside the buildings. It looked like the unit was built like a baseball field. First place was the segregation dorm. Second place was the gym connected to the general population dorm. Then, third place was F-dorm, where I would be housed. It was actually for the better acting inmates. To be housed here kind of surprised me considering I had a sex case that was to follow me here, apparently it did not.

Trustees were housed there, and the guards were to be taken far more seriously than the ones in Dayton. They meant business and had been in the business a long time. They were not young and were mostly white, unlike Dayton where they were mostly black. The guards here had faces to me. The dynamics of the entire unit intrigued me. All of these country redneck looking crackers were under the supervision of a black warden. Totally weirded me out, this disturbed my initial belief that the white guards here may not be as red across the neck as I believed. Discovery mentally noted, they seemed like just people, but seriously doing their job.

I was scared, mostly because I didn't have a way to reach my mama in case these people did something to me. I was afraid of getting raped by a guard and afraid that no one would believe me. I developed this perception of prisons from watching too many of the fake ones on television and cable. I recalled the prison film Lisa Raye was in where the guards were raping the female inmates and I just assumed this is what happens in prisons . . . I had never known anyone in the free world who knew anything about prison to get any different perception. I was terrified that I was alone. I had no one and nothing in the middle of nowhere called Hobby unit. This was a humbling experience. I made up my mind not to trust anyone. I wouldn't be friends with anyone.

F-dorm was huge. It housed about 100-150 women. It was two stories tall and looked like a huge hangar. The bunks were only separated by a three-foot wall and there were beds all up and down. The day room had two televisions no one could hear with all the noise from the fans, inmates talking, showering, and the picket bosses talking over the intercom. There were six metal tables with four connecting seats. If you kept walking straight back, you would see the bathroom. A five-foot wall separated the day room from the bathroom area. The bathroom area had eight toilets and eight sinks. There weren't any dividers between the toilets. Everyone could see you changing your tampons, smell your bowel movements and hear you pee. The shower was to the left of the toilets. There were six shower heads, three on one side and three on the other. There was nothing to separate the showers from the toilets, nothing to separate each shower from another. Any guard who walked around the wall to go up the stairs where the rest of the bunks or inmates were could see everything. I tried never to be in the shower when I knew there would be a male guard on duty.

I made up my bed and laid there staring at the ceiling. I was reclassified for this unit only to be put on the hoe squad again. However, this was no ordinary hoe squad. There were eight hoe squads and I was on squad three. It was torture. They turned the hoe squads out around 5:30a.m. Getting turned out there means you are being dismissed from the dorm to work or wherever you were supposed to go. We went to chow in a cafeteria. Everything was hurry up and wait. The guards would rush you out of the dorm only to have you wait in line some place else.

I didn't know jack about how things went and didn't know anyone who could tell me. However, the breakfast was incredible. They had pancakes with butter and peanut butter, cold water with ice and juice. It was amazing. The food was hot and delicious. I must have been too slow because, boss had this tall, dark, skinny girl named Ziggy come back in and get me. I was so busy eating I had not paid attention that every one of my squad members were gone.

I got in front of the line because my last name was Anderson.

"Anderson, what the hell were you doing?" boss screamed at me.

I said, "I wasn't finished eating."

"Well, you bring your ass out when you see the rest of the squad leave. You got that?"

"Yes, ma'am." I didn't know what else to say. I was scared because she looked old and mean and was a red neck. I felt a little better when Ziggy said, "I'ma call you the nutty professor."

And everyone laughed. I was too scared to crack a smile.

We marched out into these fields. Everyone had hoes or aggies (the regular garden hoe, just with bigger blades) straight up in the air. The palm of every hand was filled with the top of the wooden handle, leaving the blade high in the air. I could not believe how fast we were walking. I was virtually running and out of breath, but I insisted on my body not falling apart, not showing how freaking tired I was. I was sweating and we had not even started working yet. The ground was dry and rocky, the sun was already hot and it wasn't even 7a.m. Yet, I could hear the marching of the horse's hooves on the ground that the bosses were riding. Our steel-toed, black, state-issued boots crunched the reddish clay-colored dirt beneath our feet. My balance was getting poor over the moving dry clumps of clay as I struggled to walk quickly over them.

"Stop!" Tighten up my line, 3 hoe," the boss declared.

Everyone moved closer together. I followed everyone else. Ziggy ran to the front of the line. It was about 20 of us. We were now in one straight line instead of paired up like when we walked out

"Aggies in the air," the boss yelled. I could not believe every single blade seemed to be touching the sky. I had to get mine higher. There was even a wall of shade from the blades that appeared to be connected somehow, raised high in the air. I was just glad we had stopped marching so I could catch my breath without anyone making fun of how out of shape I was.

"Down!" boss yelled

Every blade hit the ground on time. You could hear the whisper of the aggies swinging in the air and the chopping sound they made on the grass below. The rhythm was almost like a cadence. Higher and higher the aggies seemed to go in the air. This sound went on for about 20 chops. And then the real fun began.

"Sing!" boss yelled

Is she serious? I didn't know the song they were singing. Ziggy started a song on the beat of the chops.

"Wanna be a . . . baller, shot caller, 20-inch blades . . . "

I wanted to laugh because was Ziggy really rapping to the sound of the blades hitting the grass.

The she said, "Step! Down! Down! Down! Step!"

That sound was almost like music.

We went on like this for what seemed like hours. The sun baking the light skinned to brown and the brown skinned to black and the black? Well let us just say I was now blurple which is a mixture of black blue and purple. The heat was immense and killing. Stifling was the still dry air to where you almost stopped breathing just because it was too hot. The blisters swelling up on my hands with fluids in little ovals, but I had to keep going. The fear of not knowing the consequences of stopping willingly was greater than the fear of my sinews ripping from my body.

My arms felt like they were being torn apart from my body. I still refused to be defeated. I was tough and could handle this. We must have stepped and chopped half of a football field before the boss yelled for us to stop. A tractor with a huge tin tanker attached to it pulled up and the boss told us to walk it off.

I was so terribly broken and tired. I could not wait to get a drink. Unfortunately, I was too slow for that line because I was last. When I got up to the watering tank, I thought *this is how they do animals . . . water them out in the fields.* Why couldn't I have a cup or a glass for water? Still on my high horse, I bent down to sip the hot outside tank water. I only had two gulps before she yelled for us to line up.

I knew we were going in. It was hot outside, and I looked around at all the grass we chopped down. For the first time, I noticed the gardens, birds and trees, and the blue sky. I could not believe I was actually seeing beauty in all of this. My hands were bleeding and the puss filled blisters had popped. The sting of the open wounds mixed with the red dirt seemed to be so minor compared to the immensely fatigued muscles in my arms and back. I could not even pay attention to that pain when I was still standing in what felt like to me 100 degree heat. My feet were burning and I could feel sweat all in my butt cheeks and between my thighs. I knew I must have smelled like a mule.

I got back in line and we headed for the unit. We stopped on a dirt road with veiny greens in different places all over the road, leading back to the unit. Against the red dirt, the veiny greens reminded me of Christmas colors. Funny how that is what I thought about. I also kept thinking that I should not have eaten so much breakfast. In fact I felt I should not eat breakfast at all if we were going to work like slaves in the hot sun all day and I was only going to get two sips of water.

I felt sick, like throwing up would be a good idea. I was dizzy and couldn't see straight. I pressed on because the alternative punishment for failing this assignment which was supposed to be something the average inmate could do . . . I believed would have been worse. I just would have rathered fallen out dead before I surrendered and vomit. Every time I felt a little come up, I would swallow the hot burning fluid back down and try to will it mentally to stay down.

"Line up!" The command came again. I thought we would be chopping grass. "Aggies down!" This time the aggies were on the ground stretched out in front of us. "Now skin it back."

I wasn't a dummy. I caught on quickly that we were to scrape the ground and the green vines of grass off the road. We did this all the way to the back gate. I must say, the road looked nice and rich and the fields were amazing.

This was the day I would never forget. I will remember for the rest of my life how they hauled us into what they called the bull pen. It was the back gate we entered through when we transferred to this unit. It must have been about 30 feet long and 40 feet wide. All of the women lined up, and some raced to be first. They checked roll again because it was count time.

"Anderson?"

"807513," I rattled off without thinking.

We stood in line, and some of the women were already naked. I could not believe my eyes. At least 100 women were getting naked. We were in line facing our boss. The first girl walked up and handed the guard her clothes. I could not look, but it didn't matter because everywhere you looked there were naked women, as the bosses checked their clothes.

It was my turn. "What's your number?"

"807513."

"Hand me your clothes, for Christ's sake." Boss scowled at me.

I was holding the clothes against my body—afraid of every one seeing me naked. I was completely humiliated, but I was at the mercy of these people. I handed her my clothes and then the worst happened.

"Turn around, bend over . . . Spread your butt cheeks. Squat and cough. Spread your toes. Turn around. Lift your breasts. Shake your hair, stick out your tongue. Alright. Get dressed." Boss growled at me with a scowl on her face.

My clothes were on the ground—my panties, my bra, and my socks. Now, I had to put those clothes on my body and be alright with it. I could not hold my head up. I followed the boots to the chow hall, but I did not eat. I threw my food away and walked to get in line. We were going back out there and that meant I would have to be searched again, coming in.

We marched out to the fields and walked to where beets and sweet potatoes were planted. We were handed burlap sacks and told to pick as quickly as we could.

"The first day here is usually the worst day. It gets better," an inmate told me.

"We're in the same dorm. My name is Sue."

I never said a word. I just kept my head down and continued to pull the beets as quickly as I could go. She followed me.

"You can talk, you know, when we come out for the second half."

"Okay," I was able to mutter without crying.

We went back to the back gate around 4 p.m. I was not even over the shock of the first strip show and now I had to go through it again. I detached myself from the moment. Still, I felt like I was being raped. I followed the feet through the gate where I was asked over and over again what my number was. Finally, I got to the sally port or the hallway that was outside the dorms, and waited to be let in.

"What's your number?"

"807513."

"Where are you coming from?"

"Work."

"Where you work?"

At this point I wanted to scream and say, *Bitch, does it fucking matter? I am in prison. None of these jobs pay shit, so who cares?* I politely responded, "Hoe squad 3, ma'am."

"Put your ID in the box," she said and slid a box out from the picket and I put my ID in. She held me up while she let at least seven other women in and then she sent my ID back and let me in the dark gloomy dorm.

"So what's your name?" Sue asked

"807513," I said sarcastically, hoping it would run her off, but she laughed like that was the best joke ever.

"No silly, what's your real name?"

"Brandy, but everyone who knows me calls me B." I said to her still not able to look at directly at her for the shame.

"Well, you either better hurry and shower if you plan on going to chow, or you could just wait 'til they call chow, but it may be soon. We go first today."

I decided to wait and about 20 minutes later, they called chow. I dreaded going for fear of stripping again, but I did not eat lunch and was starving. That night we had baked chicken, beans, potato salad and yellow cake, water and punch. I was impressed because the food was good. I don't know if it was so good because I had worked so hard that day or because it was just plain tasty. I didn't have to rush, but I did.

I made it back to the dorm and got my gown and underwear. I packed a bar of soap and two towels and trotted downstairs to the shower. I peed in front of everyone, but no one seemed to notice. I showered alone. No one came in the shower while I was there. It was dark and I rinsed my braided hair so the water could fall down my face and dilute the tears falling from my eyes.

I was not even sure why I was crying, a lot was going through my mind. I had been stripped in front of hundreds of people, told to spread my ass cheeks and lift my breasts, stick out my tongue. I had felt this way before, this shame, this humiliation that could be compared and measured to nothing else in the world. I showered recalling the night my mother did not come home to 5319 Bolivia until late. I had packed all of our clothes to go to Terry's on W Montgomery. She played for a church revival that night and did not get in until midnight. Terry's was the closest and was open 24hours. When Adelia walked in tired and was ready to go straight to bed, I walked out with the clothes to be washed, I had to because my little brother and sister had no clean underwear and I didn't get paid until that day, so I had no money to wash until then.

It was past midnight. Then it seems like there were a lot less people in Houston than there are today. No one was on the road, no one was at the dark laundry mat except someone behind a pulled down towel at the desk. There were no doors, no windows and it was poorly lit. I had washed the clothes and packing them back to the car. When I shut the back door on the driver's side, I was dragged down quickly to the side of the washateria where there was nothing but the smell of urine, broken bottles, gravel and absolutely no light. There was a knife at my throat which switched from my throat to my side as he spread my legs, breathing humid air on the side of my face. I lay silent with tears quietly falling. I could feel the small pebbles from the ground digging in my back and cutting the backs of my thighs. I imagined myself in the car watching doing nothing. He plunged hard inside of me and I just laid there smelling him smell like motor oil. I still imagined myself in the car driving away. Even with the knife to my throat, I never thought about him killing me unless I tried to fight him. In minutes he got up and stepped on my shoulder with his cheap tennis shoes leaving a foot print on my sleeve. I laid there for minutes before I got up and ran to the car, locking all the doors and driving to Courtnee's who was only five minutes away.

I knocked on her window and climbed through. She could see I had blood running down my legs and thought I had been shot or stabbed, it wasn't until she looked in my face did she know what happened. She took me to the bathroom and drew water, she took off my skirt and sandals, and I had no underwear on. She sat me in the water quietly because everyone else in her home was asleep. My best friend never said a word to me, just sat my blood stained body in the warm water and held me crying with me.

That is how I felt in this place without my friend holding me. I was feeling raped all over again. Feeling like I had to be quiet about it, no one to tell and if there was someone to tell, no one could do anything about it. I could not disassociate the fact that this stripping and humiliating experience was self-inflicted, that it was something that did not have to be. I did not *have* to be there. I should have found a way to stay at UT. I should have followed the law, should have listened to Adelia, listened to my grandmother. I sometimes thought maybe I could not hear them because I was so broken. The incident at Terry's that April of 1988 was too much for anyone to handle without words. Courtnee literally took that secret to her grave. I did not understand that this was part of prison, this was not rape. Yes there was the shame, yes there was the humiliation and yes it did feel just as sickening then as it did that night. Would I get to another level of I—don't—give—a—fuck—about—what—happens—to—me attitude again like I did after that night? I did not know, but one thing I knew for sure as I stood in the shower, just like I was never ever the same after Terry's, I would never ever be the same after prison.

I cried every single day. I was not even sure why I was crying because I knew if I were out, my life would be just as pointless and meaningless as I felt it was here. I would still feel just as lost and alone and I did here. I at least could be around more people like me and out of Adelia's way.

This was my routine for almost six months. I never made any more friends. Sue was even a stretch for me, but I could tell she was good people. The days were long and always so tiring. I ate less and less because bathing after working in the dusty red clay that stained all of my white clothing, was more important than eating. It was also quieter for rest or sleep when most of the dorm would leave for chow, so I would sometimes just eat something like Vienna sausages or summer sausage from the commissary I had in my lock box. I quit eating breakfast altogether. The food was making me sick because of having to work in the hot sun and moving around so much. I arrived at Hobby unit weighing 232 lbs. but I now weighed 170. I had given out my TDC number so many times until I sang it out in my sleep whenever they woke us up for count time in the wee hours of the morning.

I didn't write my mother as much as I had while I was in Dayton. I still had no clue as to where I was. I really thought I was being lied to when they told me the address was P.O. Box 6000, rural route 6, zip code 77666. I thought it was a joke to go along with the one about it being Devil's Island and the red dirt was like fire. I did eventually write my mother though.

Dear Mama,

I hope this letter finds you and Ed in good health. I hope that PJ and Mykala are doing well, also. I really don't know what to say. I guess I will start off with I love you and I miss you. I really have no clue where I am.

I am fine though. I have lost a lot of weight (smile). I hope Mama Duckie is good. I heard Uncle John wasn't doing too well. I will keep him in my prayers. I have never told you this before, but I do appreciate all that you have done for me. You do not owe me anything. I hope you do not feel like any of this is your fault. This new place has got me thinking about a lot in a different way. Anyway, thank you for always being there for me.

Brandy Anderson.

There was no fluff or lies or fakeness to my letter. I had no time for it anymore. I just thought it was high time I got real with myself. It was time I started dealing with things like a courageous woman instead of the scared little girl I came in as. I knew I would never be the same, but I had time to think of whom I would be when I would no longer be here, I had no idea how long it would take to create this new person. I knew the old B was broken, shattered into a million pieces and only I with the Lord's will could melt those pieces and mold a better Brandy.

These bosses were nothing nice. The inmates here were scary, they had killed people, they were older and had been there a long time. One woman had baked her baby and served it to her husband; another was there for killing her husband, and one lady was there for leaving her kids locked up in a car in the summer time, so they suffocated. Her punishment would not have been as severe if she had not been high on drugs, blocks away from where she parked the kids in the car.

I was no longer a big fish in a small pond like in Dayton and in the county. There were women in here that had killed and molested their own children. There were young women in here for repeated offenses, women who had been in here before. There were women that were not afraid of the guards and the hard work. I was afraid.

I was not asleep when the guard knocked on my bed. I was lying there, just *thinking* about reading my Bible since I could not sleep.

"Anderson?"

"Yes, sir?"

"You got a lay-in."

I was surprised because the guard did not ask to see my ID and did not ask me to repeat my TDC number. I was going to classification. I was scared of that too. I was thinking, *there must be a job worse than where I am and that's where they are going to place me. I must not have been doing a good job on the hoe squad. Was my aggie not high enough?*

I really was not going to go to sleep now. I feared the worst. I thought they were going to place me with a male guard who was going rape me. That was it. I had no idea what to think now. I was terrified once again.

I did not go to chow. My lay-in was for 8 a.m. and that meant not turning out for the hoe squad at 5:30 a.m. I went to the classification building and waited. It was the only building with air conditioning. It had all of the offices for the major, sergeant, lieutenant, warden, Chaplin, and counselors. The infirmary was also there.

"Anderson?" a man asked. He was wearing a cap instead of the usual cowboy hat.

"Yes, sir?"

"Let me see your ID and come with me." He said

I followed him to the office where a small black lady sat behind the desk. Her name was Ms. Williams.

"Ms. Anderson, I need a trustee who can go outside the gate. You must follow the strict instructions of my officer. If you are found or caught with any item you pick up while you are out there, you will find yourself with a free world case. If you continue to keep to yourself and do as you are told, you will have no trouble here. I tell all inmates to do your time. You earned it. You broke the law, so you earned it. So do your time; do not let your time do you. Do you have any objections to this?" She asked me.

I wanted to say, *Hell, yeah. I would like to object to being framed as a runaway and shot. I would like to object to being gang raped by every guard here. I would like to object to a lot of things.* Of course these were things that had not happened, just the still engraved perception of what prison was according to the films . . . in spite of the fact that none of these things ever happened nor were there even rumors of these things happening, I still was a believer that they would. But instead I said, "No ma'am." I had my preconceptions of what went on in prison like everyone else. I thought all the male guards would try to rape me, thought I would get framed for escape. I thought of all kinds of crazy shit because I was always a worst case scenario thinker and those were the worse cases to me.

She handed me a piece of paper putting me on the trustee outside yard squad. I had no clue as to what the outside yard did, it seemed like there was nothing else to do but grass and fields, all of it was outside . . . so what would be the difference? I was not excited about being a trustee. I went back to the dorm and told Sue.

"You will like it, B. It is not like the hoe squad at all. The squad is smaller, the bosses don't yell at you as much and most importantly, you get to leave the unit." Sue explained

"Yeah, but then I have to be stripped every day." By now, I had become used to the buzzing sound of the picket unlocking the doors. I had become used to using the restroom and showering with an audience, but I had still not become used to getting completely naked when I'm coming back onto the unit from work.

"You will get used to it, and they usually don't strip you out in the open. You might as well get used to being stripped. You are in prison, B. Ain't a whole lot they going to trust you for. You couldn't be trusted in the world to do right, and it is their job to make sure you ain't breaking no laws while you in here doing your time." Sue said matter a factly

As much as I did not want to hear that, she was right. Sue had gotten really sick and could not work on the hoe squad anymore. She had been transferred to dorm monitor. All she did from 8 a.m.-5p.m. was clean the showers and toilets, mop the floors and wipe down the seats and tables. Even that was hard for her because she was bleeding a lot. She was waiting on surgery for a hysterectomy. They told her it was the only thing that would stop the bleeding. I had the rest of the day off, so I helped her clean up.

I thought about what Sue had told me. She was right. What I was going to do about it, I did not know. I knew what I needed to do, but did not know if I had the courage to do it.

I went to chow and ate with Sue. Sue was like an aunt to me. She told me things in a matter of fact manner and I did not mind because she was so sweet to me and looked for nothing in return. Generally, it was hard for me to be kind in return because I had not been for a long time, but it was easy to do with Sue. She was the one person I never judged.

The next morning, I got up at 4:30 a.m., showered, and waited for them to call the outside yard squad. They did not call until 7a.m. I was quite surprised because I expected to be turned out for such an esteemed job earlier than the rest, but the real deal was that I turn out later than the rest. I was nervous, but felt like Sue was right. I deserved whatever hard work they had for me to do.

I walked to the back gate and met up with some other women in white and steel toe boots. A white van pulled up and I followed the ladies inside. A really heavy white man with a kind of pointed nose and crooked front tooth handed us safety vests to put on. He wore a cowboy hat, but the female guard who drove us wore a cap that day. She had on a blue apron over her gray uniform.

"I want you to pick up a trash bag when you get out the van and pick up all the trash you see; Cigarettes—not the butts, not the matches.

If you can see it, it needs to be picked up," Mr. Behring said. He did not scare me, but immediately I respected him. I had been around perverted men before and he just didn't seem to be one of them. He appeared to be a Christian man, a family man and a man with sound, good morals.

He talked to some of the other ladies because he knew them; they had been on his squad. I was the new boots. I wasn't going to say anything. I did okay, I thought.

All that walking gave me too much time to think. I kept remembering how mean I was in the world. I had done so many things in my life that I was now facing and ashamed of.

I carried a lot of anger and guilt for getting my little brothers, Perry Jr. and Cedric in trouble. They trusted me to listen on how the scandal would work. They trusted that I would not let them do anything that would land them in jail, and yet, they wound up in jail. How could I ever forgive myself? I was sure they never would. I could never face them again.

I would walk the highways day after day thinking and thinking, but never saying a word to anyone. I had decided when I came in not to make any friends because all the women in here were prostitutes and drug addicts. One day, I had just gotten out of the van and grabbed my garbage bag. The only people who were turned out that day were me and two white girls who were buddies. They took off walking and picking up trash behind the female guard. I was stuck with Behring.

"You know, Anderson, you can't spend the rest of your time not talking to people. You walk around with your head hung low and that ain't going to solve anything. You come out and you walk and work on the outside, but you need to take that walk and work on the inside." Stunned, not showing it on my face.

The day that Behring spoke to me, I realized two things. I realized he was not a boss, he was an officer. The second thing I realized was that I was going to be more than an inmate.

I got up the next morning actually looking forward to going out on the highway. I had his conversation on my mind all night. For some reason, I could not make myself open that Bible, not yet. I did not deserve, I had not earned the right.

Sue was taken to John Sealy Hospital for surgery. I was now alone again. Several weeks passed and Behring did not say anything to me. I guessed it was because the opportunity had not presented itself. But one day, he finally approached me. I was picking up trash, walking alone, as usual, when he caught me off guard . . . I was in deep thought about a friend from church who had been murdered with her baby who was only a month old. I wondered if the killer had ever been caught. My thoughts ran from the night my mother told me Pam and the baby I had not yet seen were dead to the day of the funeral when I saw her holding the baby in the casket at Barne's funeral home. I was thinking of how I wanted to see that baby and never got to see her.

"Do you read your Bible? Well, I guess I should ask first do you even have a Bible?" He asked me.

"Of course, I have a Bible," I answered with almost a smile.

"Do you read it?"

"No."

"Well, maybe you should. There is something in there I think you should know."

"And what's that?" I asked.

"The answer."

And then he walked off. He did not even allow me the opportunity to ask what the question was. I didn't think it needed to be asked, because I already knew.

I needed to take that walk within my own soul and do the work to fix my relationship with Christ. I walked on and on picking up trash. I started taking pride in my work. It was important to me that my assigned area was clean. I started recalling bible verses Adelia would send to me like faith without work was dead . . . I did not want to be dead, so I worked in faith, with faith that I would live and not die spiritually.

The next morning, I ate chow. For breakfast I ate a bowl of cereal and drank some juice. I figured I could handle that on the highway.

I went to the back gate and hopped in the van. As I looked out the window, I noticed we drove in a different direction. I was curious about where we were going, but it really didn't make a difference being I had no say in the matter. We pulled up to another unit. It was TYC, the Texas Youth Corrections facility. We were there to cut their grass. I was ready. It was something different.

"I want Famous to lead out with one lawn mower closest to the fence, Allen you make the second cut and Anderson you follow then in the same pattern making the third cut. You should be finished in 30 minutes. Then you got there and over there and there. By the time you get done with that, it will be time to eat lunch." Boss said

We heard the instructions and I was amazed at how beautiful the grass looked when we finished. It had appeared so patchy and ugly at first. I was impressed at the technique used to cut the grass so fast and precise.

We went to the area where the boss was. It was another grassy spot with picnic tables and benches. He told us to sit down and then a nice looking, young lady brought out a tray with white Styrofoam containers. Boss seemed to be familiar with her, but not in a nasty way, just kind of like he knew her outside of work.

"Okay, everybody grab one of these."

I was last. I didn't open mine until someone else opened theirs. In it was a grilled chicken sandwich, a bag of chips, a pickle and two oatmeal raisin cookies. The lady came back out with a tray with Capri Sun drinks. I was grateful, because although the work was fast, it was hard and made you sweat more.

"Lord, thank you for this food we are about to eat, continue to guide us in all we do in this life," Boss prayed.

"Boss, why you always pray when we eat? How you know we all Christians?" one lady asked.

"Because Christ made us all, so we all belong to Christ, making you His . . . not Houstonians because you from Houston, but Christians because you are from Christ."

"Well, I been a Christian boss; I been in church my whole life," Famous proudly said.

"Well, if you been in church your whole life, you would not be here," Boss responded. The silence lasted a few minutes because we realized that was true. Another thing that kept ringing in my head was sin keeps you away from Christ and Christ keeps you away from sin so in a way boss was right. Had we all been in church like we were supposed to be, we would not be here. Our ransom had already been paid; our debt was already clear so we had no real reason to be in prison except we had chosen sin over Christ.

That painful truth had me thinking too. Adelia had played piano for churches my whole life. I had been to every church service. Plus, I had been baptized. So, why was I here?

Boss continued, "There is a story in the Bible that says some seeds fell on rocky ground and when those seeds were exposed to the sun, they quickly burned up. The seed was the word of God. You ladies need to ask yourself, what kind of ground are you?"

From that day on Behring would talk to me. He told me that I needed to read my Bible every single day. I couldn't give a tithe nor an offering with money, but I could give what I had a lot of . . . time. I committed to that too. Behring also told me it was time to forgive myself. I was never going to get out of the prison mentally, if I didn't. He told me that I did not need to focus on getting out, and I did not need to focus on getting visits, and I needed to stay focused on the work within my soul. Stay focused on the word.

I believed him, day after day. Months had passed and he had given me so much useful advice. I read my Bible daily. I prayed daily. I was feeling better and smiled sometimes at the sun and continued to fall in love with how beautiful things were: the sky, the grass, the air, trees and birds. I had never paid any attention to these things before in the free world. I was growing content with my life on the outside yard squad.

It was the end of November after Thanksgiving. Behring called us out for work around 8 a.m. He had us picking up trash all day and then we walked to pick up pecans the rest of the day. We did not go far from the unit.

"Anderson, what do you want to do with yourself when you go home?"

"You told me not to think about home," I laughingly told him.

"See, Anderson, you don't listen. I said for you not to focus on going home. Now seriously, what do you plan to do when you get out?"

"I don't know, Boss. I think sometimes the things I wanted to do, I won't be able to because of my record. I really would like to go back to school."

"You know they have college here in prison."

"They told me this unit is not one of the units for college."

"Well, we will see what we can do. I am going to be transferring soon to another unit. Now, I have asked Mr. Hemlock to put you on his squad because you being on Dugger's squad will be nothing but trouble."

Dugger was a mean redneck, trailer trash of a boss. He believed the inmates were to be treated like men. They had to pee outside, spit and find bottles to drink water from. I was told he was cruel for not letting some baby skunks free. They were in one of the watering pipes and he could have just let them go, but instead he slammed the pipes over and over again until they fell out senseless and then he killed them by dropping the pipe on them several times. He could have let them crawl back to the woods, but, no, he killed them.

I protested, "But I heard Hemlock doesn't want any black people out on his squad. And how come you have to go anyway? Why can't you stay here?"

"Because when you grow, you have to go. Only dead people stay still, Anderson. If you do not move, if you do not work in this world, that means you are not growing, you are not doing anything. I planned on getting a position as lieutenant one day and my best bet is to transfer to a bigger unit."

"And what's going to happen to me?"

"What has happened to you since you were in your mother's womb? The Lord will take care of you. Trust the Lord to take care of you, Anderson, and He will."

The next morning, I got up to turn out for work and was told I was not turning out. I was to work the back gate that day. I was not sure if I was ready for that.

I met a lady named Marsha. She had what looked like liver splotches, but they were dark. She swept up the bull pen after the strip searches and she took out the trash. She was nice and we found out that we were both from Acres Homes, a community in Houston. My grandmothers lived off Carver St. and her mother lived off West Montgomery Rd. near the police station.

"You know why they left without you?" Marsha asked.

"No, I just thought because boss had too many people "I said looking dumb

"They got a tip that Ashley was going to try to bring drugs on the unit." Marsha told me

"That does not surprise me because Ashley does nothing but sway back and forth in the dorm and she has been quite happy these days lately." I added rolling my eyes

"Mr. Behring must really like you; he left you behind because he knew you ain't have nothing to do with that drug stuff." Marsha told me

"you really think so? I mean I don't know much about drugs except what I have learned in here, but I have not heard anything either." I said not really knowing what to say to that. I knew I had nothing to do with drugs nor drug addicts. Ashley was not my friend and I hated that glassy eye stare she would have sometimes, like she did not have soul. Did Mr. Behring really leave me behind because he knew I had nothing to do with drugs? Did he really think that much of me? And if he did why did he? I was no one special; 1 had not done him any favors. I was not like some super grass cutter he could not live without on his squad.

Mr. Jones, a tall, dark-skinned guard with blue eyes, told us to go on in. Because technically we never went outside the gate, we did not have to strip. We were about three feet away from the chow hall.

"You better hurry and eat because I guarantee you they are going to lock this place down if they do find drugs, and being that Boss sent us in this early, they are probably on their way back."

I hurried into the chow hall. I had a good feeling that she was right. I grabbed a tray and fixed it up with baked chicken, macaroni and cheese, green beans and chocolate cake. That was always my favorite meal. I ate as quickly and as safely as I could. I left with Marsha and before we could make it back to the dorm, they called count time. I went in after calling out 807513 and trotted up to my bunk. Everyone was coming in the dorm from everywhere. They came in from various jobs, Rec, laundry and infirmary. The warden ordered every inmate on their bunk for this count. So when Ashley's bunk remained empty and count had cleared, I believed Marsha was right.

We still could not move out of the dorm. They brought us Johnnies, the little brown paper sacks of food. There were two pieces of bread, a piece of chicken and a piece of cake and milk. I thought it was really cool I got another piece of chicken and cake. They never gave us cooked food for Johnnies before. I think they just didn't want to throw away all that cooked food. I was thankful. I sat on my bunk thinking of all the times I had walked with boss. I thought of how I was hurt because he was leaving. I was praying and reading my Bible daily. I was even was thanking the Lord for so many things I had never thanked Him for before.

I went to sleep reading the Bible. I woke up to the wonderful sound of "What's your name and number? And show me your ID."

"Anderson, 807513"

I changed into my gown and went to sleep. When I woke up again, I had a lay-in for Hemlock's squad. I didn't know what to think about going to Hemlock's squad. Boss told me to trust the Lord, and I trusted what Boss told me. I walked alone through the back gate. I slowly approached the shed that was about 20 yards away from the back gate. I had not even made it there and a giant of a white man with a John Deere cap and blue overalls marched out. "I told them I ain't want no more spots," he said loud enough for me to hear him. I stopped dead in my tracks and thought maybe I needed to go back in.

"You Anderson?"

"Yes, sir."

"Well, come on before the picket boss shoots you." At that point I thought it would be better to be shot. I walked up to the shed and walked in. It was like Petty Coat Junction in there. There was a woman with stringy long brown hair and a nasty tan called Williams. There was also another woman with a black hair cut short called Dusty. They didn't say anything; they just looked at me like I had just peed on myself and kept on making coffee. Why on earth were the inmates making coffee with a real coffee pot ? Where I had been coffee was instant with tap water. I just sat there until I was told what to do. He assigned everyone something and somewhere except me.

"You ever had a garden?"

"No, sir. my great grandmother had one . . . I have seen one."

"Weeeeelll, you are about to learn how to plant good seeds in good ground. You gone learn how to respect these fields. They gone teach you things you will never forget. Come on, Anderson. I reckon I better do my job, even if I don't want you out here. Hell, you here now."

I don't know where I got the strength to say anything more than I already had, but I finally asked, "Why don't you want any spots out here? I ain't no trouble."

He looked at me puzzled. I couldn't figure out if it was because I had the audacity to ask him a question or because he really didn't think I heard him when he called me a damn spot.

"I allow the ladies out here to have a few free world things. They drink coffee, I bring them bacon sometimes and what I do not want is any of the stuff I do getting back to the unit and then the next thing you know, I am having my butt hauled in for fraternizing with the inmates. And the last time it happened was with a big mouth black girl," he candidly said to me. I could only return the kindness.

"Well, I am a small-mouthed woman. I quit being a girl when I got a job in the free world. So I guess we better get on out here and learn whatever these fields have to teach."

"Hop on the trailer." I rode with him out to the very fields I chopped down when I was on the hoe squad.

"This here is barley, the other field is wheat" he said pointing and directing my view to various areas on the massive unit. There is a time and season for everything we plant to grow. The things we grow take nutrients from the earth, so we got to put some back . . . planting the wheat, barley and rye gives back the nutrients to the earth." We drove on around to another field. "Here we planted tomatoes, and there we planted jalapenos. Come on and let me show you where the water is. Every day you are gonna water something. Over there in that field are the onions. When all these crops come up, we have to let it be for six months to a year after you grow the rye, barley or wheat.—depends on what you plan on growing next. You have to be consistent with the seeds. You have to be attentive when the weeds grow and pluck them out right away so they don't stunt the growth of your seeds nor your crops. Never let weeds destroy good seed." He romped around the fields and walked and talked with me following behind.

I listened and I thought he was talking like boss. Mr. Behring always said we were like rocky ground; good seeds were planted but the ground was not prepared to receive it. Was boss Hemlock saying that too, a time for everything . . . not letting weeds destroy good seed?

He pulled out his pocket knife and swizzled it around. I was not impressed, because I still had not figured out whether he was going to cut me or if he was trying to be funny. I just starred. He pulled up a sweet potato and sliced it in half. Then he sliced a piece thin as a potato chip and told me to eat it.

"I don't like raw food."

"You should always eat food you grow. Now, granted you ain't grew this, but I still want you to taste it."

I grabbed the piece of sliced sweet potato. He sliced himself a piece and ate it. "Mmm, mmm! Now that is gon' be a darn good potato. Anderson, you ever ate a baked sweet potato?"

"No, sir."

"Well, it is the sweetest thing you ever could eat. Hop on." He grabbed up a few of the sweet potatoes and we headed back to the shed. He started a fire in a barbeque pit he had on the south side of shed next to another shed. He wrapped the potatoes in foil and put them on the pit.

"If you want, you can either go in and eat lunch, or you can stay out here and eat off the land."

I had eaten the sweet potato chip raw and it was good. I was up for the challenge of staying out with the big old, nigger-hating white dude and "eat off the land," as he put it. He had a small fridge in the office shed. He reached in and pulled out a bottle of water. I drank the water and it was so good. I drank the bottle straight down.

"If you think that's good, you need to try some well water. It's what all the crops are watered with."

"Well water from the ground?"

"Hell yeah, now that's better than spring water, better than purified water . . . just wait. We going to go get us some tomatoes and onions and jalapenos. I got some hamburger meat and cheese and bread. I'm gone put this meat on the pit while we out there."

I followed him to get the stuff. He handed me the mayo and lettuce and cheese and a package of foil containing the hamburger, cooked and smoked to perfection. I ate mine with no bread. It was the best lettuce, tomatoes and jalapenos ever. Then came dessert. He unwrapped the sweet potatoes and poured a little honey on it after he slit it down the middle.

He pulled out the butter and put a pat on the potato. He handed the hot package to me, still in foil. I opened it to find the savory butter all melted. I grabbed one of the plastic spoons like I was welcomed to do so and spooned up a piece. Incredible. It was sweet and buttery, with a nice, smooth texture. I was used to cooked down, sugared up with vanilla extract, flavored dices. This was nothing like it. It was so much better than what I was used to.

I would never eat in the chow hall again. They always served cooked food, never a fresh salad or fresh fruit. I stayed out there with Boss until the sun lay down. I finally turned in around 6 p.m. I felt a new spirit. Was it the food? Was it Hemlock talking to me about this and that? Was it the sunshine and less stress, or just a combination of it all?

I sat on my bunk and read my Bible before I even showered. I was too grateful for everything. I was too grateful that Hemlock's bite was only a bark. I was grateful he liked me after all; at least I thought he did.

I took a shower and when I was done they called me to the picket for mail. My dear Adelia had written me.

"Thy word is a lamp unto my feet, a light unto my path," was written on a small piece of paper.

Dear BB,

I just wanted to drop you a few lines. I am in Chicago right now on assignment with the I.R.S. Everyone is fine. I hope this letter finds you well. Ed is here with me and Mama is doing okay. She had been sick and I plan on taking her to the doctor when I get back. Everything is fine.

I am glad you are reading your Bible. I appreciate you being so thankful, but I am your mama. I am never going to abandon you. I love you, BB.

You are my first-born child. I see no fault, nor shame, in you. I have never wanted you to feel like you were the black sheep. No one is holding you in contempt; we forgive you . . . now, you need to forgive yourself.

I have sent you some pictures of Olivia. Perry thinks he's going to get married.

I am going to sign out now. Oh yeah, I have been talking to the warden and some other people about getting you transferred closer in, hopefully to a unit where they have college (smile).

Your mother loves you. Jesus loves you.

Mama

I cried for so many reasons. I cried because at that moment I realized the Lord had been watching over me since I was arrested. I had been so ungrateful, so oblivious to what was really going on in life. The Lord loved me, my mama loved me and I had been clueless all these years. For so long, I had been angry about the circumstances of my life. I was angry because of the financial deficit of not having child support, angry about stuff and with people who did not matter, and angry because I did not have the love of my father.

Anytime I called my birth father, Craig, I cussed him out. I was still hurt from the time he passed right by me, stopped to make sure I saw him and then the bastard drove off without saying, "Hey, B.," or "Hey, you want to go with me?"

He and my mother were divorced when I was 6 or 7. My baptism was the last time I saw or spoke to him, until that first call, when I was 16-years-old. He never called me, I called him. He always told me he never bothered to come and get me or check on me because my step-dad, Perry Earl, told him he would kill him if he came around. As true as I believed that may have been, I still felt Craig's sorry ass should have felt his first child was worth dying for. My mother would have felt that way.

I showered and went to bed facing the wall. I prayed my mother or no one would ever come to see me. I was too ashamed to see them.

Boss and I walked around the fields every single day for weeks. He talked to me more than he did the none spots. "You have to take good care of your fields, Anderson. You have to keep focused and stay on track with your fields. Focus is very important in life as well. You have to always know how to separate your good crops from the weeds. Weeds will sneak up on you and before you know it, they are choking all of your good crops out and although they were doing so well and growing so good, they will die. I guess I have taught you enough, Anderson, to let you have a key to the tractor. When you come out tomorrow, I will have you a key hanging on the hook. I am going to trust you with these crops. I have shown you how to take care of them. You take care of these crops like you are taking care of yourself. You got it?"

"Yes, sir. You can trust me; I will take care of them."

"If you kill these crops after all the time put into them, it will be very, very bad. They will die and you will be right back here starting over."

"Yes, sir."

I got the message, the whole message. Take care of myself, stay focused and do not let weedy people suffocate my growth. If I didn't learn that message, I will be right back here in prison . . . working these fields.

I turned out the next morning and there was my very own key to the Case tractor. I drove out to the fields assigned to me and made sure there were no weeds. I made sure I watered when it was time. I walked and romped around the fields checking on the crops and eating all I could of the fresh grown delicious cantaloupe, tomatoes, jalapenos, and nectarines that grew where I wasn't assigned, but allowed to go. I did a fantastic job. I know because the crops grew well, nothing died as months went by. It was now time to move on to new crops, for the new season.

"Anderson, it's almost summer time, and we can't do too much in the summer because it gets so hot out here, sometimes. The most we can do is cut the grass with the Kubota, because they don't turn out the hoe squads when it's too hot," boss told me. Then he asked, "So Anderson, what are you going to do when you leave this place?"

"I was hoping to go to a unit with college. I already have some college. For as long as I am probably going to be here, I may wind up getting a degree or close to it."

"Yeah, I had heard about you trying to go to college. We will see what we can do about that."

I thought to myself I *'ve heard that before.* When I look back, when Behring and Hemlock told me that, they probably didn't send me because I was not ready. The Lord did not allow me to leave Hobby, because I was not ready.

I realized though, I had come a long ways. When I arrived, I was afraid of Devil's Island. Now I was in control of growing good crops . . . on Devil's Island with all that red dirt. I was no longer concerned about where I was in Texas. To this day, I do not know where Marlin, Texas is. I learned to be more concerned about where I stood with the Lord.

I read my Bible every single day. I was halfway finished with the Old Testament. I prayed so much until I prayed more than I talked to people. I prayed when I went out for work. I talked to the Lord every day and I walked around the fields. I talked to the Lord and prayed and thanked Him for everything that came to mind and things that did not. I prayed in the shower and just thanked Him. My hair was growing so long, I felt like it was time to get a perm. I put an I-60 in the mail to the beauty shop. They made an appointment for me for July 2, 1999. They would not let me see myself in the mirrors. The real mirrors were only for the guards. I looked at the vision looking back at me in the tin they allowed inmates to use as mirrors. I was just satisfied to be done with asking people to braid my hair every other week. I didn't feel right anymore trafficking food in from the fields where I worked like I secretly had been doing for so many months. I would bring in stuff like jalapenos, pecans, onions and cherry tomatoes for the trade of getting my hair braided. My hair was long enough to put in a pony tail. It was high up on my head, hung past my shoulders and it bounced. I felt cute even if I could not see it.

My mother wrote me a lot and she was sending me postcards from everywhere she traveled. I was getting more mail than anyone in the dorm. She wrote me from Kansas, Nebraska, Illinois, and other places. I had these wonderful photos from all over the United States to look at and I would imagine myself going there. I was so proud of my mother. She was taking care of my little sister who was now in high school. She had my brother to look after because he had a mental illness that had not been diagnosed nor treated previously. It took several hospitalizations and episodes later before he was diagnosed with bipolar disorder. She was taking care of her husband who had a stroke and could no longer work and my grandmother Mama Duckie who was suffering from a perforated colon, not to mention she was 90-years-old. She had her brother John, who was also ill with congestive heart failure. Uncle John was her favorite brother because like her, he also played piano for a church. I could not believe how she was taking care of all those people, and she still found time to write me. One particular letter explained she and Ed would be coming to see me soon. I was really hoping not. I sent her a letter and told her to check before coming because we may be on lock down and they will not allow visits during that time. I could not face my mother. I was still too ashamed. I was her first-born child, the oldest who was to supposed set the example of what to do in life. I had graduated from S.P. Waltrip with honors from the International Baccalaureate program. I had gone to the University of Texas. I had been the smartest one of all the grandkids. Everyone said my little cousins looked up to me, and held me in such high regard. Now I had failed them all, but mostly I failed God and myself. I begged the Lord for forgiveness daily. I asked for forgiveness from my family on every letter. It got to the point where my mother did not even respond to it anymore. I fasted on weekends once a month as a sacrifice to say I was sorry to the Lord. I took pride in my work because I knew I was doing my time and not letting my time do me. I stayed focused. Getting a visit would only put me off track. I could not face my mother knowing now that I had failed her so miserably with my foolishness.

She did not care I was a lesbian. That took some counseling and a lot of conversations between us before I realized this just before I was arrested. She cared that I knew the Lord. She never cared if I wanted to go to college—she cared that I made good decisions to be self supportive and happy. Believe it or not, I was happy when I was in the fields. Taking care of the crops was my only focus, my only goal and anything more than the Lord at that time, would have been too much for me.

Sunday came and Hemlock gave us the option to turn out on weekends if we wanted to. The church service I had planned to attend was not until 3 p.m., so I got dressed and went to the picket where I pushed the button for the guard. "Yes" the guard replied in a why-are-you-bothering-me-so-early-on-Sunday-morning voice.

"Uh, yes ma'am. I was trying to turn out for work please?"

"What's your name?"

"Anderson"

"What's your number?"

"807513."

"You know you have a visit?"

I wanted to ask her, *how the hell would I have known I had a visit if you ain't told me?* "No ma'am."

"Well, you have 15 minutes to do whatever."

I ran back upstairs to see if I had a uniform that wasn't so ratty, that wasn't so discolored from the red dirt. I was trying to see if I had some underwear that wasn't colored with red or a bra that wasn't discolored. I put on my Rhinos. I had bought a pair of suede, tan Rhinos from commissary a few weeks ago so I could have something other than my ruddy work boots for church. I was making such a fuss over the visit and had talked all that noise just a little while ago about not wanting to see my mother, but I could not believe it . . . my mama was here.

I had kept a new pair of underwear and a new bra in the back of my lock box. I put on my best uniform and brushed my hair up into a nice and neat pony tail. I slid on my boots and ran downstairs.

I pushed the button expecting a delay and verbal harassment, but the guard just buzzed the door and I went on out. I walked on quickly to the visitation building. I was asked to put my ID in the bucket where the picket was. The guard raised the bucket and I was in the walkway waiting anxiously. He lowered it and I walked in the building, where I was told the rules: "no kissing, no holding hands, no hands under the table, you must remain seated during your entire visit or you will be sent back to your dorm, no . . . no . . . " The guard rattled and all I heard was all the no's until I was sent to another room to strip. On visits, you strip before and after and you can't use the restroom except in your own dorm when your visits are over. You can't get up. Yet, I was so excited. I hoped that I looked as nice as I could look in a TDC, all-white uniform.

"Mama!" I screamed and cried out when I saw her thin body standing up and looking for me. I walked and hugged her. She held me so tight and then pushed me away. I sat down at the table. Ed came around and gave me a strong hug.

"I have missed you guys so much!"

"BB, you have lost so much weight. Are you eating?"

"Yes ma'am. I eat nothing but the fresh foods from the gardens most of the times. How is everyone?"

"Well, Uncle John is not doing too good. I am surprised that your Uncle Sonny has been right by his side. We are making it though. Mama is doing better. She had a virus and was sick, but she's fine now. I have been trying to get you transferred closer into Houston or at least to a unit with college."

"Yeah, have you been getting your money?" Ed asked.

"Yes, sir," I replied.

"Ed, would you get some snacks for us?" my mama asked, all nice and lovingly.

"Yeah ." Ed got up from the table and walked down a short narrow hallway to the vending machines. He stopped to pay a guard $2.00 to take a polaroid snapshot of us for after the visit.

My mother told me how she did not want to see anymore letters where I was begging her for forgiveness. She had forgiven me a long time ago, the Lord had forgiven me a long time ago and it was time to forgive myself and move forward. She wanted me to think about what I wanted to do with my life when I got out. I was still not convinced I was ever getting out. She talked to me like I was not in prison. She was so happy to see me, Ed was happy to see me, too. My mother's voice was low and still I could hear every word. I listened to her for the first time in a long time. Before I knew it the visit was over. I didn't ask for anything except a good-bye hug.

I watched them vanish opposite the door where I was headed. I don't remember the strip-search, I don't remember the long walk back to the door. I did not come back to the real world until the guard hit the buzzer to let me back in F-dorm. I did not want to be in the dorm. I knew I would only think about how much I missed them and I would do nothing but cry. The last thing I recalled from the visit was them walking out of my life and I could not go with them.

"Can I turn out for work? Please? Boss said I could come out late."

"I will call and check. You go on in though until I call you because it's almost count time," the guard responded. I was glad because that meant the girls in the dorm could not bother me with questions about the visit. I did not want to talk about or even think about the visit. I changed into my jumper and changed my shoes. Lying down, I waited for count to clear.

It only took ten minutes. I grabbed my ID, gloves and hat and headed down the stairs.

"Anderson to the picket to turn out; Anderson to the picket to turn out for Hemlock's squad," the picket guard said over the p.a. system.

I was already at the buzzer and walked on out. I walked quickly to the back gate and showed my ID. I couldn't wait to get out there. I trotted to the shed, where Boss was on the phone. He pointed to the keys and I grabbed them, running out to the shed. I jumped on the Case tractor and took off for the okra field, which was the furthest away from the unit. When I got there, I jumped out and marched to the well to turn it on. With every crunch of dry earth beneath my boots, I dropped a tear. I was weeping by the time I reached the well and was dreadfully crying by the time I headed back to the tractor. Even with my eyes blurred and flooding, I could see Boss standing about 15 feet away by the tractor. Someone else had driven off in the Kubota. I wiped my face and just hung my head.

"Hop on, Anderson," he said in a steady voice. I hopped on the trailer. More tears fell as I bounced. We pulled up to the shed. Boss had seen the distraught look on my face when he pointed to the keys and decided to save me from whatever disaster could have happened.

"Let's have some coffee, Anderson," he suggested.

"Okay," I said. My eyes were swollen eyes.

He really didn't have to say much to let me know he cared. He said, *I am sorry you are hurting,* with the way he handed me a cup. I felt him explain, *Things will get better,* when he poured me a cup. Every spoon of sugar, every ounce of creamer was like a pat on the back. We sat and drank the coffee in silence for a few minutes, but it seemed like hours.

"Anderson, you will be leaving this unit soon. I want you to never forget these fields, never forget what you learned here. I want you to do well when you get out. Never forget to read your Bible every day and pray every day. Trust the Lord will always protect you, if you are living and doing right. Never forget these fields, because if you do . . . you will be back to see, they will always be waiting on you."

"Yes, sir. I will never forget and I will never be back."

I got up and he noticed I had blood on the back of my pants about four inches from my waist band. He looked closer and said, "Anderson, how on earth did you not know you have a tree poking out your behind?" he pulled out his knife and twisted it all around like he had before. I smiled and he told me "Let me take a look at it, my granddaughter got one of these last week and I was able to pull it out."

I pulled my pants down those four inches. Over the last few months, I learned boss was no pervert. He was just a good old country boy who tried to make life a little bit easier for folks who weren't going to snitch him out. I trusted him. He pulled out one splinter, the largest one and told me the other was too low for comfort and it wasn't sticking out. I ran my hand inside my pants over the other splinter and it was deep inside my skin. I wasn't worried, although it did hurt.

"Well, Anderson, the sun's about to go to sleep on us. I'm going in."

"Okay, boss, I will see you in the morning."

He was locking up the shed and I touched his arm just below his shoulder. "Thanks, boss."

He didn't say anything. We weren't supposed to touch them, but I wanted him to know I was grateful. He never asked about the visit and he let me turn out for work and stay as late as I needed to. He didn't say anything at all, didn't even turn around, but I heard him . . . I heard him in my heart say, *You're welcome, Anderson.*

He jumped in his pick up when they let me in the gate. I could see he drove to the okra field and turned off the well. Then, his truck vanished behind a cloud of dust.

Again, I do not remember stripping or even the walk back to the dorm. I just recall taking a long shower and crying in the dark alone. I went to bed around 8 p.m. and read my Bible, lying down facing the wall so no one could see me crying. I do not remember falling asleep.

Moving again-5

Once again in the middle of the night, I got a knock on my bunk. "What's your number and show me your ID," the voice demanded.

"807513."

"Pack your stuff, you're leaving." I thought it was a joke. Boss didn't move that fast.

I must be going to Devil's Paradise since I had already been on the island. I didn't care where I was going. I just packed and waited for them to call me to turn out. I never answered the whispers of the girls in the dorm. They called my name and just like that, I was put on the Blue Bird and on the road.

It was daylight and I could see things coming into view around me. I saw cars, trucks, buses and vans. They all had new shapes. I was used to the square models of vehicles had when I was arrested in 94. Now in 1999, all the vehicles were oval shaped, and they had more curves instead of the angles.

I was amazed that I was actually in a city, now. Marlin was literally in the middle of nowhere. We walked for miles picking up trash off the highway and I never saw so much as a Flying J's. Now, I saw a Dairy Queen, a McDonald's, a Pizza Inn, and a school. At a red light, we pulled up next to a school bus full of children. I missed children. I remember I had wanted children now what seemed like a long time ago. One of my cousin's childhood neighborhood friends had always called himself liking me since I was thirteen. I would never give him the time of day until I got to Marlin and he found me. As I rode through the city, I thought of the correspondence we had where we talked about getting married and having children. He was a good man, that Vernon. He was big and strong, he was thoughtful and even in prison, he somehow managed to send me money and send books and other items. His letters were always filled with positive things to say. He told me how he had dated this light skinned woman who left him and went to Atlanta to be with another woman. I thought how sad he must have felt. I would never leave him. I was going to try to change everything about myself including being a lesbian. I did not know how that would work out, but I was sure that if I could do Vernon would be the best man to do that with. He never judged me; he was patient and so understanding when I could not write back right away. I thought of all of the secrets we shared, so many things from our pasts that no one would ever know. I loved him as a man who loved me. I don't know if I ever told him. I cant even say to this day if I had known he would die before his 35th birthday, I can't say that knowing would have changed my mind. I just thought of him as we rode through this new small town.

I looked around ten minutes later and saw more units, mountains, hills, and valleys, but I didn't see a field. .A sign on one of the units read "Lane Murray," and another read "Gatesville." Ah ha! I was in Gatesville, Texas. I did not know where it was, but I had at least heard of it. We pulled into the unit farthest from the busy parts. The unit looked older and the sign out front read, "Mountain View." The set up was pretty much the same, except everything seemed to be one story and all the buildings looked like they were made of wood and had been painted white.

There were women in white uniforms everywhere and everyone seemed to be moving fast. The guards looked a lot nicer and the women there seemed happy. I saw people walking around, smiling and talking. They seemed to be moving about without any problems or harassment. The place seemed harmonious. I didn't get a sense of tension like at Hobby, but maybe Hobby appeared to be full of tension because I was afraid when I arrived. Either way, this place already seemed way better than the one I came from and I didn't feel nor see anything devilish about it. The name had a nice ring . . . Mountain View, considering the view of all the mountains. I was actually excited to get off the bus and see what else there was to this city of women's prisons in the middle of a city in the free world.

"Unload and wait where the guard is," we were ordered. The bull pit of this back gate was just like at Hobby. There was razor wire everywhere on both the top and the bottom of the fences that surrounded the compound. We were not stripped outside like I was used to, and when they did strip us, they didn't strip all 25 of us at the same time. I was grateful for that.

They marched us to an air-conditioned building where there were other ladies already there. A big, wide-mouth female named GG just kept talking and sassing the guards. She was there to see some big time guard or the warden while the rest of us waited to be classified. I received my lay-in and followed the line going in the same direction. The guard was dropping people off at duplex-like houses. There weren't any speakers or buzzing pickets up high. The inmates opened the doors themselves.

I was housed in dorm A2, the trustee dorm. It seemed like almost everyone was a trustee. That saddened me a little because at Hobby, I thought of myself as being special. Here I would be like everyone else.

I went to bunk 23 where I was assigned. No one was there except a guard at one end of the house. There were only about 25 beds. To my left were these white metal benches and a television. There were only about five benches and you could actually hear the television. I could not believe it. There were lights that the inmates turned on and off. There were windows everywhere. We slept to the right. My bunk was a 6 by 4 foot cubicle. There was a window over the bunk across from me. When I sat down and looked out of that window, I saw three crosses with a tall one in the middle. They were sitting on top of a hill. I made my bed and set up my hot pot, radio and alarm clock. I put everything else in my lock box.

When I looked over in front of me, I recognized a small space sitting higher than where we were. It was the picket. The officers there actually sat in between two houses or dorms and watched all night. I could not believe that there were restrooms on the right of the picket with walls and curtains. Privacy when you pee? I had to go to the toilet just to see. I went in one of the stalls with the curtain pulled open and I closed it. There was a wall that went from the ceiling to the floor on my left and on my right. The curtain made it just that much cozier. I didn't really have to pee or anything, I just had to check that out.

I came out of the stall and to the left of the picket were more stalls. They too had walls. They turned out to be individual showers with curtains! I was going to have myself a private shower yet. They called lunch chow. I followed every one out of the dorm, still surprised at the inmates opening the door. They counted us when we left and took down bunk numbers instead of always asking for your ID.

For chow, they provided us with chicken fried chicken with an incredible crust, diced potatoes with butter, green beans, water and punch with ice. Everyone ate and talked in hushed tones. No one rushed or hurried to eat. No one waited at the door for a line of their dorm mates or coworkers before they could leave. They walked out on their own to their perspective places.

I could not believe I was trusted to walk back to the dorm alone. Sure, there were guards everywhere, but they let me walk alone to the dorm like I was a person. I was trusted to go where they told me to go on the unit and go there without a line.

I opened the door and noticed that the dorm had a water fountain and freaking air conditioning. I would sleep tonight in the cool. I was also going to have light, and would no longer be in the dark like at Hobby. I was in a house, not a barn.

"Anderson!" I heard someone with an accent calling my name from the front door.

"Yes, sir; I am Anderson."

"Aren't you on the outside a yard squad?"

"Yes, sir!"

"Well, come on; let's go. You are holding me up. I have about 20 minutes to be at the civic center and get it cleaned up . . . Let's go . . . Let's go!"

I grabbed my hat and gloves and went out the door, following my new boss, Mr. Garcia. He was about 5 foot 4, but stood very tall and walked very fast. His skin was very dark brown and his head was topped by a bushy halo of hair coming from under his hat which he always wore. He also always wore shades. I followed him to the back gate where I was led to a white van like the one Behring had.

There were women already there, ready to work. There was an Asian named Ly; a Hispanic mixed with German named Ruiz; an older woman named Chapa, who was always giggling about something and she had been locked up since 1968e that was before I was even born, hell before I was even thought about. Craig and Adelia had not even gotten married yet. We were a true melting pot.

I was surprised that there were no safety vests and Boss drove the van alone with no back up. No gun. No shot gun. That led me to believe the women could not have been violent or else they would not let them leave the unit with a man who appeared to have little security.

We rode through town and I was glad. We passed more restaurants, motels grocery stores and car lots. This was the world I had been a part of for so long, and now I was on the outside of the free world looking in. I was so grateful to God for being able to see things that I could not hear the women talking to me. I had no clue what awaited me when we arrived at the civic center, there was no shed for lawn mowers.

"Let's go. Anderson. You take the women's restroom, Chapa you have the kitchen, Ruiz the activity room. Mop it and clean the tables. Ly, men's restroom," Garcia said.

Everyone got out the truck. I was a little paranoid, thinking all this freedom was a set up for me to wind up with more time. I followed the women into the center thinking, *If I get in trouble for being in this free world place, I hope these women will tell the truth and say I was told by this man to go in here.*

I grabbed a bucket of cleaning supplies. I was actually holding Pine Sol and Lysol. I saw Ly go in one restroom and I assumed the other door, with a sign that had "Women" on it was where I was supposed to be. It was a bit of a mess. I put on the huge yellow gloves from the bucket and got to work. I had missed cleaning my own place in the free world. There is something slightly rewarding about cleaning your own house to me. When I cleaned up Telise's house it just felt like something that needed to be done, when I cleaned up my own place, it was like therapy. I would have time to think or focus on one thing although I was doing something else. I finished and was on my way out of the door when something caught my attention. A huge floor length mirror was on the back of the door. It had been five years since the last time I saw myself in a mirror.

I stared at the person on the other side for minutes and it seemed like hours. She was beautiful and strong. I had definition in my arms, and for the first time in my life, I had abs. I had a great smile and most important to me, I had beautiful, long black and shiny hair. I looked in my eyes and I did not know the person I was looking at. This was not the person who entered prison, I recognized the eyes, the features, but the soul I was looking at in my eyes, in those eyes in that mirror was looking back at me. She was looking at me with a smile like she was happy and different. Was this me? Was I happy and if I was what the hell for I was still in prison? Maybe I wasn't imprisoned in my mind anymore; maybe I wasn't imprisoned in my spirit or emotionally. I recalled a bible story when Paul was in prison and he said no matter where he was, he would be content. As I looked at this changed Brandy in this mirror, I realized that is exactly what I was . . . content.

"Let's go. Let's go, ladies," Boss yelled out to us.

I grabbed my bucket and went out to the activity room where they were placing chairs back under the tables after they swept and mopped. I followed the ladies to the kitchen where Chapa was eating cookies. The other women also joined her.

"You know, Anderson, we bite the cookies; we usually don't bite the people," Chapa said with a chuckle. The others laughed also, joining her in an innocent ice-breaker.

That did it for me. I smiled and they asked me what unit I belonged to. They all seemed surprised when I told them the difference between

Gatesville and Hobby. They could not even fathom having to use the restroom in front of the entire dorm. They couldn't see how stripping outside did not violate some kind of inmates' rights, considering there were picket bosses with binoculars. I never thought about that really. I wanted to talk to them some more, but for crying out loud, there was a whole world out there I had not seen in four years. So, I continued to look out of the window.

When we left, the van did not head back to the unit. We pulled onto a winding road behind a sign that read, "Raby Park." I was amazed at its beauty. There were hills and twists and winding roads. A little creek flowed on its own winding course through the park. There were tall trees and walls made of flag stones—and swings; I have always been fond of swings. We pulled over and stopped.

"Get out," was all Boss said and we did what we were told. He walked around and we followed him. The women were talking and laughing low. He walked up to a man he called Mr. Peterson, who was sitting in a white City of Gatesville truck. Boss told us to wait by the restrooms and to check them out to see if they needed cleaning up. I, of course, had no clue where they were, so I followed the women.

They checked into the restroom while I looked at the creek and watched the tadpoles swimming there. I wondered if there were fish in that creek and where it emptied. I also wondered what Boss was talking to the city man about. I just could not understand all this freedom and trust while out in this free world.

Finally, we loaded up in the van. I quietly continued to look at everything around me. We made it back to the back gate far too soon for me. We unloaded and the four of us were strip searched. I was glad I didn't have a lot of people to show my behind to this time. The guard checked our clothes very thoroughly and quickly.

Ly was going on and on about how she had curves and how her sister was just thin without curves. She was a nice enough looking petite Vietnamese woman. I was surprised to see a woman from her culture in prison. I'm sure they get in trouble too, but I've never seen one in any of the places I was locked up. She was fairly educated, although she didn't have a degree. She talked a lot, but was nice enough. She even went on about the fact that she was a lesbian.

I did not want to hear about Ly's life on the outside. I was not interested in having a girlfriend in prison. I just wanted to know more about my job. Would I get to drive a tractor? Would I cut grass? Would we be going to the park all the time? Chapa had been there the longest and told me the answers to my questions were all "yes," except for the tractor. I was excited.

I went into the well lit day room and watched the Lifetime Movie Channel. I could not believe it; they had cable. I sat there watching some movie with Jasmine Guy as a navy seal's wife. He murdered her and used 50 gallon garbage bags to line the crime scene before he killed her. This dude really covered his tracks. There was nothing those blue lights could pick up, there was no body. He also covered himself and his shoes in garbage bags, so even when they checked. Needless to say, he was a white man. Steve Harvey once made a joke about the news, how he could tell what ethnicity the perpetrator was just from listening to the crime . . . well that was one of those crimes. Black people would not care about wrapping themselves up in garbage bags to make sure no DNA was found on them, would not have meticulously taken the time to calculate how many garbage bags would be needed to cover the killing circumference or diameter area and the walls to ensure a DNA free crime scene . The crime scene investigators tried to use ultraviolet light, yet they could not find even a spec of blood. She was missing for weeks and the bastard got away with it. Never remembered the name of the movie, but it was so interesting the things they show on television in an effort to entertain or inform the public. What someone fails to realize is that sometimes you can give too much information. Like I never had seen how crack was actually smoked until I was forced to watch the film for A.A. and the 12 step program. I thought they would especially reserve those films for who??? That's right, crack users and should have had a program for check abusers, I felt even though they wanted me to take all those drug addiction classes, they opened my eyes to things I had never seen before. I could not help thinking that the same thing was happening with those killing movies . . . they were either showing slightly experienced or maybe killing curious inmates how to kill and get away with it or how to not get caught the next crime they try to commit.

The show was interrupted with a Crime Stoppers message. They showed a reenactment of a crime from 1981. I was worried about that. I did not want to see the reenactment of my friend Pam's murder on television. She was murdered in 1983 after giving birth to a beautiful baby; her daughter, Tashonna, born July 2, 1983. They were both snuffed out one month later on August 2. I did not want to see that on television so I decided not to watch anymore. At first I did not understand the purpose of showing convicts Crime Stoppers . . . their crimes were stopped when they were arrested. I later discovered that there are actually a lot of inmates who are in prison for one crime and they confess to someone else about another crime for which they have not been caught.

I sat on my bunk and a guard came in and said, "Count time." There wasn't any yelling. I pulled out my ID, but they just asked me to repeat my number. That was how they did things. I was fine either way. I sat on my bunk and looked out the window at those crosses again. The light from the street was shining on the telephone post in the middle.

I took a shower in that wonderful private shower with curtains. Then, I laid down on my bunk and listened to my radio after reading my Bible. The nights seemed so long and before I knew it, I was asleep.

The next day, I shipped out of the dorm at 7:30 a.m. with my coworkers. We traveled every day to some place new to me for a week. We cut grass on one day at a park or some other area of the city, cut grass and picked up trash at the baseball field the next. We cleaned the park another day, and the civic center on another. We were all over the place doing odd jobs. Our main places were the baseball field and Raby Park. We went there every week, no matter what. I really enjoyed leaving the unit.

There was a moment we had to cut these huge trees and once they fell, we had to cut them in smaller pieces and load them on the trailer to shredded or chipped. I loved that job the most because it was repetitive lifting giving my arms a chance to bulk up and tone. I got to cut one tree one time, I was not supposed to mess with the chain saw for obvious reasons, but I was determined to prove to boss that I could do it. Now if I would have cut off my leg or arm, I honestly don't know how I would have been able to explain that where boss would not have been in trouble, but I would have figured something out. We hauled off tree after tree and when all of the trees that were damaged, leaning, broken or struck by lightening were gone, so were we.

We later started cutting the lawn for the Warden. Her home was nice and the yard was big enough, but it only took two people to cut and edge everything. So boss put two on the garden, to plant flowers and pull weeds while two cut the grass and edged the yard. When it came to be my turn on the garden, unfortunately there were a lot of weeds. Well, me with my smart self, I took some of the Round Up weed killer from the baseball field and brought to the Warden's for her garden. I diluted it although you could not tell. I sprayed the solution all over the 12 X 6 pad of weed infested dirt. We were supposed to plant flowers the next week, we tried . . . they died. So boss tells us to wait another week, we planted again the third week later, they died. It took almost three months and digging some of the dirt out and replacing it with new fertilizer before anything would survive after that industrial strength round up. I felt terrible, but when I look back on it, that shit was funny as hell. I had killed the Warden's garden trying to kill some damn weeds. We just kept going back week after week trying to get anything to live a week. That Round Up is truly a weed killer.

My mother mailed me a letter telling me I should be coming home soon, but I never entertained the thought. She told me Uncle John had passed away and Perry had an episode and had been placed in the psyche ward at Ben Taub Hospital. I hated hearing that news. I didn't know what to do besides pray and read my Bible. What else could I do? I was used to being able to help my mother with the little kids and now she had to deal with her brother's death and the little kids all by herself. I tried sending encouraging letters, but I felt that because I was not there to help carry the burden, a letter was not going to do any good. She would tell me how money was getting tight and she had to ask Craig to send me money, which I despised, my mother should never have to ask him for something I felt he already owed.

I would start writing the letters and then just throw them away. In my mind, I kept saying that one day I would get the words right and have something meaningful to say. I knew how I felt, just could not get the words to match how I felt to come out on paper. I finally decided to do what Adelia would do, I sent a bible verse. I mailed her Psalm 70 1-5 in my best handwriting. My mother always loved my handwriting. I did not know what to say, but I knew or felt with that verse considering what she was going through, somehow she would have some comfort knowing if she felt like He was not there, He was coming if she continued to call on Him.

Weeks passed and the administration posted signs to sign up for college, a class called Boundaries, Kairos, (a prison ministry for offenders incarcerated in maximum or medium prisons worldwide) or church. You could even sign up to borrow movies from the church. I signed up for all of it. I tried to get as much education as I could, not to look good for parole, but for myself. I knew I would not take the time to try and develop these skills in the free world. There, I would not take the learn-how-to-be-a-better-me class. I knew that I had not played enough with kids my age, did not go to parties, and came from a somewhat verbally and physically abusive home. I was aware that I was not like other people and I wanted to be as close to normal as I could get.

Poor Adelia. She still sent letters about coming home. She would send Bible verses, such as Psalm 121:1-2, "I will lift up mine eyes unto the hills, from whence cometh my help. My help cometh from the LORD, which made heaven and earth," and Matthew 17:20, "For truly, I tell you, if you have faith the size of a mustard seed, you will say to this mountain, 'Move from here to there,' and it will move; and nothing will be impossible for you."

I just never thought about going home. I just tried to stay focused on my work and all of the things I could do, like college.

Ly was pretty persistent about getting me to touch her. It had been a long time for me, years in fact, and if I had just stayed away from her and stayed focused, I would have been fine. But she was moved to the bunk right next to me. She told me all about Diane, her free world partner in the world. Diane kept writing her about getting back together. Ly showed me money order receipts, along with the letters, proving that she wasn't lying. What she failed to realize is that I did not care. I did not care about her lover and I did not care she was a lesbian; I did not care about any of that stuff when I had bigger fish to fry. My cousin J-Rock was sending me all these letters from his unit in LaMesa with all of these gang signs I did not understand and hard time trying to figure out if he was telling me was going to kill me or if he thought he already had . . . I don't know, but it bothered me because the post marks would be a month behind whenever I got them. I wondered why. It wasn't until after Ruiz told me about her death row pen pal writing her and Cassidy's pen pal a guy named Renegade who was a gang member on the same unit as my cousin . . . they too were getting mail considerably late.

I had registered for psychology and economics. Ly took the psychology class with me. She was trying to get closer to graduation, too. She had led everyone to believe that she already had a bachelor's degree. I found out the truth when I went to her associates degree graduation. I was still proud of her for finishing.

Whenever the weather was really bad outside like too rainy or storming or too hot, we field hands had to stay inside. Most of us were not used to being at home during a weekday and would pretty much sit on our bunks and tell stories about things that had happened in the free world. Aaahhh that free world . . . the stories were endless.

Cedric, my play brother, would say that people sitting around shooting the shit always unconsciously play what he termed as a game called, "Top That." This would be a game where someone would say something that may indeed be a fact, and then someone else would say something more grandiose than the first. Like for example someone would say, "in the free world, there is no way I would be eating no ramen noodles. I had to have my rib eye steak every week. Then of course the second person would state, "well I have always been a veal person myself and if I had veal, I had to have my lobster on the side . . . I mean that's just how I rolled in that free world" Honestly I have heard ridiculously conversations like this. Because no one knew you in the free world and probably never will see you out in the free world, you could be whoever you wanted to be in prison.

One lady named Pamela swore she was Tamela Mann's sister. One little stud who did indeed look like Kirk Franklin was allegedly his sister. The list was endless.

Well, when we stayed inside, most of us like Ruiz, Chapa, a girl named Cassidy whose bunk was across from mine and myself would play Top That. Needless to say that Chapa would always win. We were glad to lose to her too. She could tell stories like nobody's business and we believed every word. There was this one time, it stormed so bad the lights went out in the middle of the day. I started telling a story about the time when I lived at Pearl street co-op in Austin. We shared the duties in the coop to keep the cost of rent down. It was my turn to cook lunch and I was supposed to cook hamburgers. Well I had to cook for the vegetarians also. There were these boxes of falafel left on the counter. I read the instructions . . . basically add water. I put the hamburger patties I had seasoned with garlic, onion powder and minced shrimp on one side of the grill and on the other side I had the falafel . . . they smelled wonderful. Well at noon when it was time to eat, the vegetarians were eating the falafel and talking about how good it tasted, how flavorful it was . . . and then people started getting sick. People were vomiting and had diarrhea. "um B when you cooked the falafel did you cook it in a separate pan or did you put it on the grill with the meat patties?" the shift leader asked me . . . " well hell, how was I supposed to know" I told the dorm "why the hell they ask me to cook hamburgers with some damn falafel any way?" everyone laughed for several reasons . . . none of knew what the hell was in falafel and another reason was because no one gave a damn what was in falafel.

"well one time me and my husband went to the movies." Chapa started out saying with all eyes and ears glued in her direction. "I was all dressed up and had my high heels on. My husband had gotten us popcorn and drinks. I was walking in all sexy in my heels trying to be all prissy getting my seat. It was dark so I had to walk slow. I did not know there were people on the row behind us. The lady in the seat directly behind mine had her feet in the fold of MY seat. So when I sat down, she stood straight up and she was screaming. I had broken all of this woman's toes . . . cause see she had her feet in the bottom of the fold of my seat . . . hehehehehe and when I sat down hehehehe she stood up.hehehehe" Chapa told us how she broke this all of this woman's toes with the theatre seat in 1962. Everyone was crying laughing which over powered the storm outside. We all had our own visual of this poor woman with her toes in Chapa's seat, visioning Chapa all dolled up and trying to sit all proper in the seat only to break all the woman's toes.

We sat up all night telling these stories whenever we could like on holidays and when the weather was bad or on Friday and Saturday nights. We had become like a family. We would argue, we shared things, we cried together and we laughed together.

It was late one night in September. We were not going to work the next day. Ly and I sat up talking about our free world exes and decided that we would be friends after we get out of prison. I liked her, she was cool and smart and funny. I trusted her and believed pretty much whatever she told me except that we found out she was married . . . to man . . . in the free world . . . and her husband had been to see her, not Diane.

"B. I want your hand inside of me," she said looking me straight in the face, right after talking about our exes. The picket boss was flirting with someone on the other side and thought everyone on our side was asleep, except for the two of us. It was around three in the morning and count had cleared. I was still in shock about her demand. I sat there for a few minutes trying to decide if she was just saying it because it was a fantasy or if she was serious about where she wanted my hand.

"Uh, Ly, what are you talking about?" Before I could finish my next thought she grabbed my right hand that was resting on the wall that was to divide us. Then, she pulled up her dress and literally sat on my index and middle fingers. I could not believe how willingly my hand reacted to her. She rocked and humped with her eyes closed until I felt a small amount of fluid wetting my fingers all the way to my palm. She then put my hand back over to my side of the wall. I needed to wash my hand.

After that, I was used pretty much for her pleasure anytime she wanted to relieve herself. She considered us together—I considered us coworkers who used each other and claimed to be friends.

My real friend was Ruiz. She always told it like it was. There was no changing her. She gave me my first job. She would pay me to wash her clothes and I was able to quit asking my mother for money, since she had so much going on already. Others called me her slave and her bitch. I did not care. I was not stealing, I was not offering other services for what I wanted and felt pretty good to feel like I had a job or my own little business. When my mother was able to send money, I didn't have to spend it.

One night, they called me for a letter. I could tell it was from Lisa because she used the blue stationary; She used it every single time to write me some horrible "I hate you" letter. Telise just wanted to tell me how horrible it was for her on probation, the humiliating things she was going through. She hinted that she missed me and the girls missed me, but no word of reconciliation. She told me she had a lot on her mind she wanted me know about some things that happened in the past with us. I felt I already knew. I knew and understood why she cheated on me, lied to me and I was okay with it all now. What I could not erase or come to terms with was how she was cheating with Esther on me and then she sent Kathy to the county to come take my car and house keys from me. I still had items in my possession that I could have released to her, but not her damn lover! I was floored that she sent her to see me. I still remember that old woman saying "can't we just take the car?" I just got up from the visit chair and left since I could not knock the hell out her with the glass separating us. I was like it is not the car . . . it was MY blue dodge Daytona. My favorite car in the world and I would let it go to the pound and rust to death before I let her lover drive around in my favorite car.

Ly had gotten a lay-in that night for parole. I tried to enjoy the possibility of her going home any day. She got an FI-1. That was her parole answer. That meant she could leave literally any day. I was called also, but I was supposed to see the commissioner in October 2000.

I read the letter from Lisa. She wanted to get back together. She sent photos of her children and told me they missed me. She went on and on about how she was sorry, and how she still loved me. I had heard it all before. Lisa was my true love.

"So, when were you going to tell me that you and your ex were getting back together, huh?" Ly asked.

She just went off. She was yelling like she was really jealous about the letter. I could not believe it. I said nothing because she was really pissing me off. She kept putting her finger in my face and yelling.

"That's enough, Ly," I said.

"Oh, it's enough when I say it's enough. You have been cheating on me." Now we are in freaking prison, could someone . . . anyone tell me how the hell you cheat on someone in prison with someone who is not.

How the hell do you cheat on someone who is married to man in the free world and has a lover she talks about endlessly? Made no sense and I was already fuming about recollecting on the past with that Telise.

I got up and walked into the television room. She followed me. She was still embarrassing me. I turned around and swung at her head, hitting her forehead. We both were shocked.

I had not hit anyone besides at Hobby when I knocked a girl out with my aggie. It seemed like so long ago. I was placed temporarily on another squad because Mr. Behring was sick. The lady boss I was placed with had a squad of nothing but women who loved to talk shit and fight. I was not trying to fight because that is automatically a reason to take away your trustee status. This girl kept saying things about me and I did not even know her. She kept talking and talking about how I must be doing something with boss in order to be the only Black inmate allowed outside the gate. So standing there, I quickly swung my aggie and struck her across her head while everyone was occupied watching a fight going on down the way. The girl fell instantly. No one ever knew it was me, because no one saw me. It never occurred to me I could have accidentally killed her. I still would not have said a word, scary isn't it.? She just kept talking shit about me and she did not know me. I was just fed up with all of her comments about what was I doing for these white bosses to be the only black person to get outside the gate, to get This whole scene reminded me of the aggravation I felt just before the aggie dropped. I really had just snapped. I hate when someone tries to make me do something. I felt cornered again. I had walked away and here she was following me telling me crap that was not true, hell it didn't even make sense.

Ly was livid and hurt. I finally got her to shut up. I felt terrible though. I did not want to hurt her; I just wanted to be left alone. After she went to her bunk, Ruiz came and told me I was wrong for hitting her, but she was definitely wrong for following me after I clearly told her that was enough.

"You guys will be fine. Just check on her later," she said.

Ly had a bruise on the left side of her head, and yet she still stood by me for chow lines, sat next to me in class, and went to the restroom with me. I was so ashamed of myself. I never spoke the words, "I'm sorry," to her, but I did a lot of things to show her that I was sorry. She accepted. Boss saw the huge knot and somehow knew I was guilty.

"Anderson,"

"Yes, sir?"

"I do not want to see you back in here. The stuff you do in here reflects what you will do out there, and fighting is never the answer."

"Yes, sir."

I was really embarrassed now. I was too ashamed to even tell Ly I was sorry. I just pretty much kept quiet. I promised myself that I would keep in touch with her when I got out.

The last day in September, we went to Raby Park. We were given hamburgers from Dairy Queen with onion rings and an incredible shake. I ate everything. We didn't have much to do because the leaves had not fallen yet, and the grass was not growing. Mr. Peterson drove up and got out with a cake. I thought it was for boss's birthday or something. He took the lid off and it was a good luck cake for me and Ly. I could not believe it. I just could not believe it. Ly was definitely going home, but me . . . I barely had a date to see the commissioner.

The next day, Ly was gone. Just like that. I sulked and sank into a depression. I guess it was actually going to have to be one of those things I would never get over.

Everyone thought they would send me home next. I was in disbelief. I had failed once again. I had quit fasting, praying and reading my Bible while Ly was there. When she left, I went back to all of those things. I went to all of the church services. I even received a prophecy from a man who told me "the Lord had turned his face for a moment, but in a little while he would shine his glory on me."

Another church passed out mustard seeds. I had never seen one, but was told all I needed was to have the faith the size of a mustard seed and I could move mountains here at Mountain View. I thought that was a little weird for them to say. When I got to the dorm, there was a letter from my mother. The Bible verse she included had the words, "If you have the faith the size of a mustard seed, you can move mountains." I sat up every morning and looked out the window. I told those mountains to move. They would not, so I kept saying it day after day in a whisper. The days and nights passed. Still the mountains didn't move. It takes time I thought to myself . . . and time was what I had plenty of.

We did not get anyone new on the squad to replace Ly. We were all pretty quiet now when we went out, and there was no sign of my leaving. I saw the commissioner late October and did not get an answer. Now, it was November. I told myself I should not have gotten my hopes up, but every morning when I sat up from my bunk, I still told the mountains, "move!"

We went to Raby Park one day, just to fart around. The boss didn't want to be on the unit. We really didn't either. The town didn't need any grass cut, the baseball park was closed and the civic center had no planned events because the events for Thanksgiving were moved to an outdoor venue.

The walls at the park were made of stones and boss was walking on top of the wall while we followed him on the lower part of the land. He turned around to say something, but I don't think anyone ever remembered what the hell he said. The wind was blowing really hard that day, and when Boss turned around to talk to us, his cowboy hat flew like a kite in the wind. Chapa quickly chased after it and even caught it, but it was far too late. We all looked up at Boss to discover he was crystal bald in the middle of his head. It took everything we had not to laugh our butts off. We were confused, shocked and amazed! We loved Boss and we were loyal to him, so we waited until we got to the dorm to laugh and we did not share with anyone else what we were laughing about.

My mother wrote again to tell me to remember to have the faith the size of a mustard seed and I could move mountains. I always knew that the moved mountains meant the obstacles in your life. For example, if you are short of money to pay bills, your mother coming with $60 dollars to help is moving the mountains. I never thought real mountains moved.

Time passed and I got a letter from Ly. I also got a letter from Lisa and a letter from my brother for the first time in the six years I had been there. I really was glad to hear from him. I was glad to see all the mail, but I was surprised that I didn't receive anything from my mama. Two weeks passed and still there wasn't a letter from her. I was getting a little worried because I had written her and Mama Duckie four or five times without a reply. I was not going to harass her when I did not know what was going on. Someone else could be sick.

I went to work with boss and he barely said anything. He didn't even look at me. I wondered if he were mad at me. I also wondered why he would be upset with me. Guards I barely knew were speaking to me.

It was December 5, 2000, and I saw the first death row inmate walk away from the unit. They told all of us to turn our heads close the blinds and be very still. I could see her. Her hair was white and cut short. There were two guards on either side of her holding her by the arm. She did not seem to fight or struggle. She seemed to be at peace. I arrived back at Mountain View moments before the execution of Karla Faye Tucker in 1998. She was the first woman executed in Texas since 1863. I had seen Erica Shepherd who was next to go. The weird thing was I did not know who any of these women were. I did not know their crimes so to me at the instant of seeing her, kneeling down over the flower bed with her own personal guard watching her every move. She turned around as our squad approached and she smiled at me. I still think about that smile and how she was going to die and still she smiled. I still don't know why she was there for capital murder; she seemed like a female you would meet at the bus stop. I was there when Jessie Jackson visited her. I did not see him, but I do recall the hoopla about his visit.

We had cleaned death row once. We mopped the halls where the guards were, about four feet away from the first cell of death row.

I could barely sleep that night thinking of how I saw Betty Beatts leave, knowing she would never return. She had been convicted of killing several husbands and burying them in her back yard. She had collected insurance money from them all. I focused on the crosses and prayed for her and the victims. My morbid thoughts ran wild thinking of what her body looked like after she died, wondering if she just slept or if there was any pain. Wondering if there would be any victim's families there to watch her die. I don't think I could watch someone die even if they had killed someone in my family. Strangely I wouldn't mind killing someone, but I could not watch someone else kill someone and watch that person die. I thought of what must have gone through her mind when she killed her first husband, and then the second, and how did she go to sleep at night knowing she had snuffed out a life of someone who had not beaten her, nor raped her. In my mind those were good reasons to kill someone was if they had done something really terrible to you or your family. I wondered had she had any children for any of her murdered husbands. I wondered if she had children what her children thought of her, what kind of mother was she if she was apparently not the best of wives.

I looked at those crosses and just thought about how she had damaged lives and compared it to every person in my dorm—all the lives destroyed or hurt at the very least because they were not home. I thought of all of the people I in my family I hurt and had lost while I was in jail. My uncle John and my Aunt Effie passed away first. I got the letters and seemed like they weren't dead to me because I was not there to see to them dead. I didn't go to a funeral, didn't see the programs. I had no closure so to me they were never dead.

I laid there on my bunk and thought about Sue, Boss Behring and Boss Hemlock. I thought about how they were genuinely concerned about how things would be for me when I went home. They watched over me when I was so scared of the alternative to them being my boss. I laid there and I thanked them. I thanked the Lord for putting them in my life.

I do not know when I fell asleep. I only know that when I was awakened, it was 4:50 a.m. The guard knocked on my bunk and said, "Anderson, pack your stuff, you're going home!" I had not been fitted for free world clothes, I had not spoken to my mother to come and pick me up. I had not coordinator where I would be paroled to lately . . . these are the general things that you discuss like weeks before you are discharged. I had listed my mother's address on Deep Forest as my paroling address, I guess they verified the address with Adelia and she must have agreed. I did not cry at first, I don't think I thought it was real after all this time.

The whole dorm jumped up out of their sleep, any time anyone got to go home or leave these walls everyone was genuinely happy for them. Everyone wanted to see just anyone go home and not come back . . . . Go home to your families, go home to your new life, and go home to your new future and new ideas. It is amazing how in such a hopeless place, hopeful faith still survived.

I looked down at Ruiz who had shared songs with me, danced and played with me, laughed with me . . . and made my time so much easier to manage. She came down to my bunk and hugged me tight. Still I did not cry, still I did not think any of this was actually going to happen.

I left everything, the hot pot, the radio, the head phones, socks, tee shirts, gloves, hats, visitation whites (which was a prison uniform that was brand new you would keep for just visits) I gave away every single thing, except the letters people sent me. I gave away pretty much all I had in my box,, from can openers, cans of sardines, cans of tuna, numerous soups, corn tortilla chips, Zapps potato chips, Bud's Best vanilla sandwich cookies, hot cocoa, squeeze cheese and fritos. I would no longer need them where I was going. I could not believe. it had been six years and I was finally going home.

They chained us together and Blue Bird flew us to the Gatesville unit. I was fitted in a clown suit of colors and wore my rhino boots home. After signing some papers which were papers telling me what things would be in direct violation of my parole, things telling me that I would get something called gate money a total of $50 dollars upon arrival at parole, there was some clause about accepting this privilege and understanding that there will be no trial next time, straight to prison and all of the free time I have spent in the free would be lost time. I basically understood that if I had 4 years left on parole and violated parole on the eleventh month of the fourth year, just one month shy of making if completely off paper . . . I lose all three years and eleven months and would be in prison starting that same four years over again. I had seen so many women start over and over. A two year sentence turned into ten years because they get out on parole every two years and screw up on the eleventh month of the second year and wind up doing another eighteen months in prison and going over that cycle over and over again.

, I was told to appear in front of my parole officer in the morning. I had to report to some address on 43rd St. which was about four miles from where my mother lived. I knew exactly where it was because I took my Uncle Cat there once. Even with all of this, I still did not think this was real, but I continued to go through the motions and do whatever they told me to do. They had us lined up and then taken to another room where we were seated at a long rectangular table with connecting seats. It was cool inside and there was no air conditioning. They called a roll and my name was first on it,

"Anderson?" I almost cried then because I was able to answer "here" instead of 807513 . . . I was called by my name instead of a tap on my bunk and told to spill out the numbers I had been recognized for years as. I was then escorted through a gate—and this time I did not have to strip. I did not have on white, no steel toe boots. I did not have to worry about whether it was count time and if it would be okay to walk through that gate. I could see myself in slow motion, getting closer to the guard who had called my name, I could see the sun shining from the crack in the doorway I was passing through and still I did not cry, I still did not think this was really happening. How could it? I had convinced myself no one ever leaves; they would never send me home.

As I kept walking, I thought of the bible story where Sarah turned into a pillar of salt because she looked back. She looked back because she missed something in all the chaos she was told to leave behind, she missed something in all of the destruction, and she missed her past. I wasn't going to miss a damn thing. I was not going to miss the blisters, the aggies, eating fast, stripping fast . . . getting dressed fast.

I would not miss the hard labor, I . . . Brandy Anderson would not look back.

I was certain my mother was already aware that I was being released or they would not be letting me go and I was right. There she was, in Perry's new Maxima with Ed, waiting for me. I ran to my mother and hugged her. I cried and gasped for my first deep breath of free air. I was hugging Ed and Adelia and still did not seem like this was real to me. I was getting in the back seat, still not real to me. The radio was on, I could feel the leather seats, the seat belts . . . it is amazing the things you never paid any real attention to when you were free, but when you have been locked up and free again . . . you notice all kinds of things, like mirrors, fabrics, smells and the way things feel to you is like all brand new.

As I got into the back seat of my brother's Nissan Maxima, I was still in awe of being with my folks and leaving. But as my mother drove the opposite direction—away from Mountain View, I knew it was real. I prayed as we drove off and told the Lord, *I know you are not supposed to look back, but I just want to see it for the last time.* I turned around and almost fainted.

"Mama . . . Mama . . . Look. The mountains, they are moving!" I said with tears rolling down my face, as Ed continued to drive. The mountains got smaller and smaller as we drove further away and finally, there were gone completely.

LAST WORD

Those mountains are now 13 years behind me. I am sure someone somewhere is saying yeah right move mountains, but the amazing thing to me about the bible is it is a lot about interpretation or perception. I saw the mountains really move, I know if no one else did that I whispered to those mountains not just the real ones at mountain view, but the mountains of anger, the mountains of grief, regret and pain. I watched those mountains move further and further away from me, out of my life and soul just before I lost it. Those messages, the words of course are not all verbatim from what the bosses told me, but they did indeed tell me these things. People look for miracles to be something loud and boisterous for everyone to make a spectacle. Jesus was a miracle baby from a miracle birth and he was quietly placed in the back of a motel with animals in a make shift manger. I saw and still see those bosses as amazing people who listened to the word of God when I could not hear Him.

My cousin Derrick once said when we were older and could laugh about the whippings we would catch, "Oh yeah you gone mind somebody." I am glad nothing horrible happened to me. Did horrible things happen yes, I still recall a woman who fell on the concrete and was having a seizure during a shake down. We were all instructed not to help her, to step over her and keep walking. There were rumors of guards sleeping with inmates but I never actually witnessed any of this myself.

My mother, my dear sweet mother still plays piano and is the greatest mother in the world. My sister is happy living her life by my mother's side. My brother is happily married with a beautiful wife and three handsome sons. Ed passed away as did Mama Duckie. I lost more of my friend's right after I got out. My mother played for Courtnee's services which to me were unfair to her extended family. Courtnee and I had buried Precious and I lost the best friends I ever had in my whole life I honestly thought I would have my whole life. I grieve daily over Courtnee the most because her death was sudden to me. I carry her picture with me every single day because I never want to forget the one friend who chose to love me unconditionally with no strings attached, without judgment.

Ruiz and I worked together for years. She had all of that time and I did visit her when she was still locked up and I got out She is my best friend and I love her family. I watched Ly graduate, I was very proud of her and still am. She will never know how sorry I was to hit her and will never know that I miss her. We heard that Chapa was finally paroled somewhere in Lubbock last year, we could not find her. I don't know how old she was, but anyone who spent over thirty years in prison ain't still young, if they are even still alive considering she had been in thirty years thirteen years ago. The Countess is still in my life and she always will be. She is the one constant thing along with my great friend and captain save them Erika, who loved me enough to make her first daughter, Cedrika, my God-daughter.

I visited Vernon quite often. I loved him and he asked me to marry him. I decided to because he had then become my best friend. He had so much understanding and love for me how could I, even a lesbian, turn down someone loving me for life. He did not care if I still was attracted to women, did not care if I still had "friends" . . . he told me he was really sick with congestive heart failure and wanted someone just to take care of him. I agreed to do so when he came home. We never got married, he never came home. He passed away from congestive heart failure two days near his birthday 2004. I was there to bury him as well.

For a while with so many of the people from my past passed away from aunt Effie, uncle Dave, uncle John, mama Duckie, Precious, Courtnee, Vernon, Perry Earl Sr., and Ed all back to back I wondered how long I was going to live. Did I make it out only to die soon? I just figured my time was running out and I did not want to waste any more of it. I wanted to live and give my all and everything *in* everything I did. Whatever piece of them that lived in me, I wanted it live as best as I could. I would love everyone, forgive all and understand all I could understand and accept the things with no explanation as just those things I was not *to* understand.

Lisa still lives in Dallas. I who just came out of a very bitter and terribly heart breaking break up, could not handle our distance as friends. I still love her; she always had the sweetest kisses and will never be forgotten. She gave me a gift once when I was feeling really invisible to the world, she saw me when I felt no one did. She gave me a gift and I will forever be grateful.

Telise still lives in Texas City. She wrote me a letter exactly ten years after I was arrested. I still have that letter today. In the letter, she told me how she wished she had not messed up our relationship with some of the decisions she felt she had to make at that time. She explains in the end, she did love me just had a "messed up way of showing it." She is now a grandmother of a beautiful little girl. Her two girls, my first set of children are doing fine. She has a degree and is still striving for better things. I only wish her the best.

Did I ever find that one woman who would be my partner forever? Of course and like Telise who messed up with cheating and lying to me so did the white girl and the last ex whose children were my life. I honestly would have laid down my own life for one of those children, even to this very day I still miss my kids. In my heart, they will always be my kids, my E.Berry, my Ricky-do and Scoota-boo.

I live around the Houston area now and there is a prison not far from where I live. Every now and then I will recognize a gray-uniformed guard standing in line at the Wal-Mart on Wilson and the beltway, or I will see a Blue Bird on the highway with the tin over the windows. I say a prayer for them under my breath, for the guards to be good stewards and be the bible some inmate somewhere will read. I realize all things came together for the good of those who love the Lord, just like the Bible said it would. I still have mountains, we all do. Again life is about perception, do you see a mountain's beauty? Or do you just see it as an obstacle? something in your way. See the mountains, talk to them, there is a reason they are there. When you know how to move your mountains, you no longer see them as being in your way; you no longer see them or perceive them the same.